EVEN MORE BAD PARENTING ADVICE

GUY DELISLE

TRANSLATION BY HELGE DASCHER
AND ROB ASPINALL

Thanks to Nadège for accepting to be the "bad guy" in my stories.

Also by Guy Delisle:
A User's Guide to Neglectful Parenting
Jerusalem: Chronicles from the Holy City
Burma Chronicles
Pyongyang: A Journey in North Korea
Shenzhen: A Travelogue from China
Albert & the Others
Aline & the Others

www.guydelisle.com
www.drawnandquarterly.com

First paperback edition: August 2014
Printed in Canada
10 9 8 7 6 5 4 3 2 1

Library and Archives Canada Cataloguing in Publication
Delisle, Guy, author, illustrator
Even More Bad Parenting Advice / Guy Delisle.
ISBN 978-1-77046-167-3 (pbk.)
1. Fatherhood—Comic books, strips, etc. 2. Parenting—Comic books, strips, etc. 3. Graphic novels. I. Title.
HQ756.D443 2014 306.874'2 C2013-908476-2

Drawn & Quarterly acknowledges the financial support of the Government of Canada through the Canada Book Fund, the Canada Council for the Arts, and the National Translation Program for Book Publishing, an initiative of "Roadmap for Canada's Official Languages 2013–2018: Education, Immigration, Communities," for our translation activities.

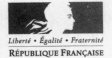

Liberté • Égalité • Fraternité
RÉPUBLIQUE FRANÇAISE

This work, published as part of grant programs for publication (Acquisition of Rights and Translation), received support from the French Ministry of Foreign and European Affairs and from the Institut Français. Cet ouvrage, publié dans le cadre du Programme d'Aide à la Publication (Cession de droits et Traduction), a bénéficié du soutien du Ministère des Affaires étrangères et européennes et de l'Institut Français.

-Math

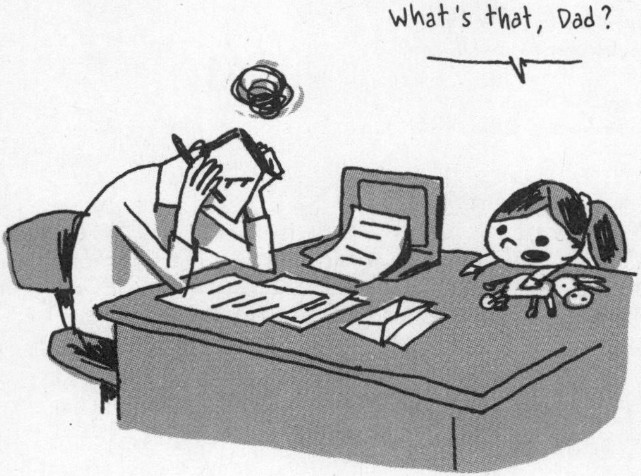
What's that, Dad?

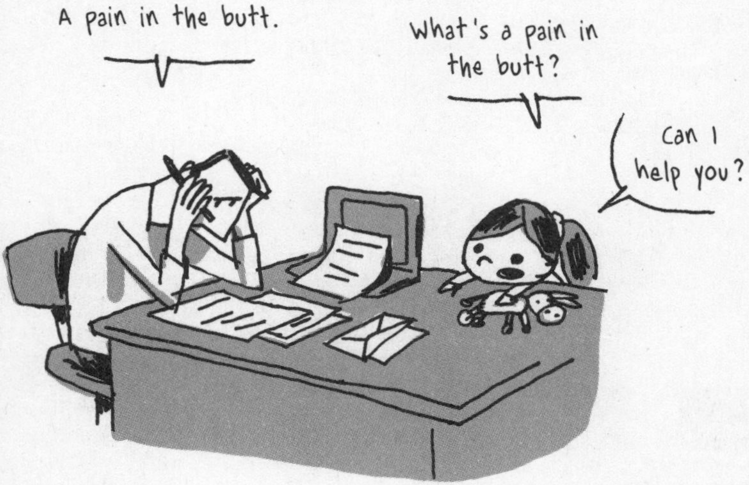
A pain in the butt.
What's a pain in the butt?
Can I help you?

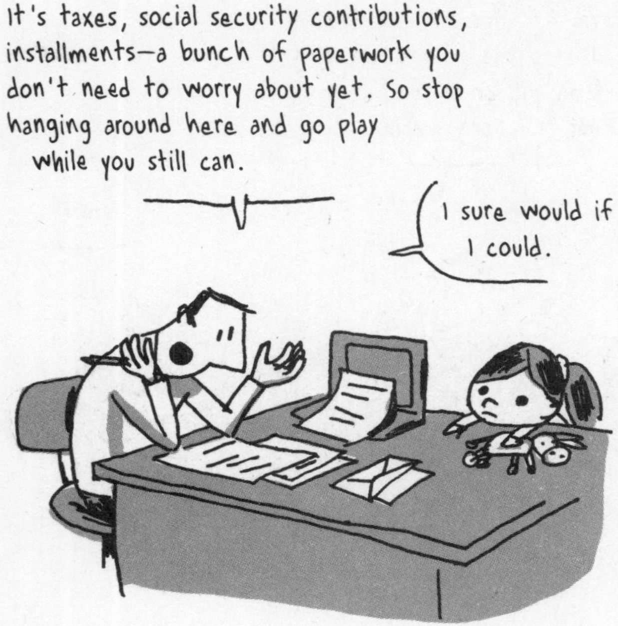
It's taxes, social security contributions, installments—a bunch of paperwork you don't need to worry about yet. So stop hanging around here and go play while you still can.
I sure would if I could.

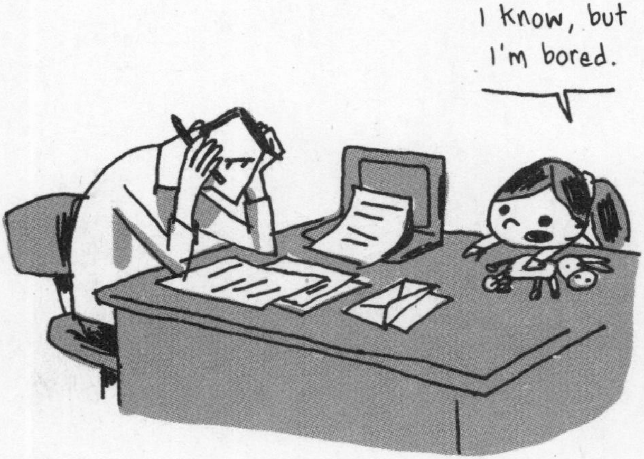
I know, but I'm bored.

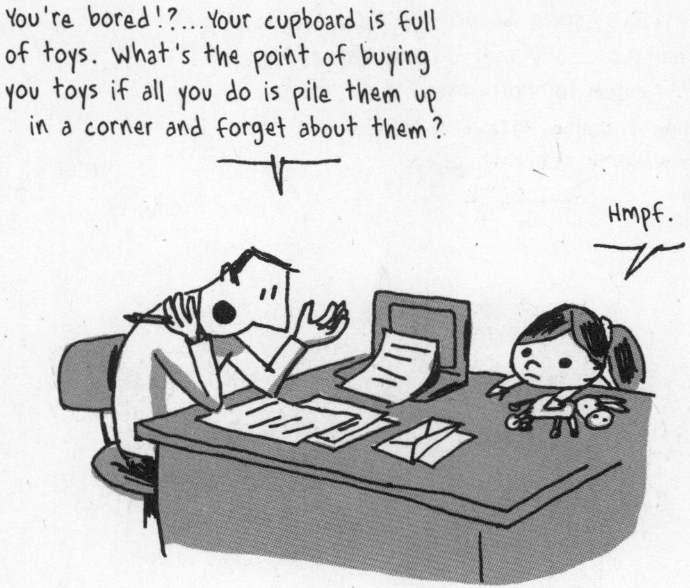
You're bored!?... Your cupboard is full of toys. What's the point of buying you toys if all you do is pile them up in a corner and forget about them?
Hmpf.

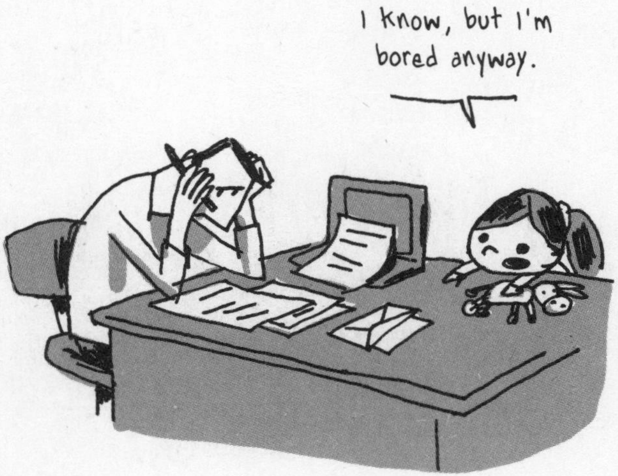
I know, but I'm bored anyway.

Well, if you don't want to go play, you can empty the dishwasher...Or how about you do some math? You got a lousy mark on your last test. A bit of extra practice wouldn't hurt...

Anyway, leave me alone please.
I need to concentrate.

Hmpf.

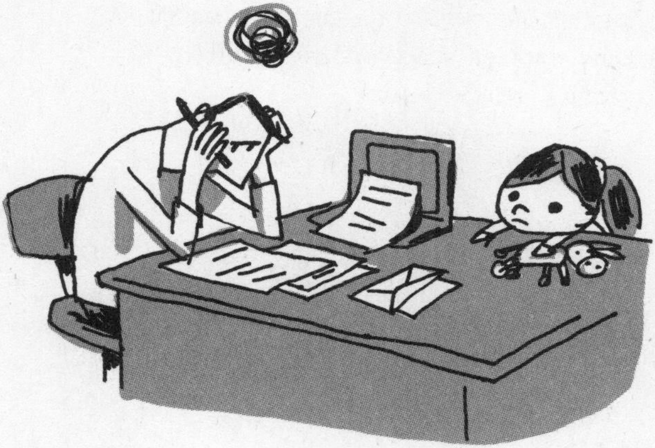

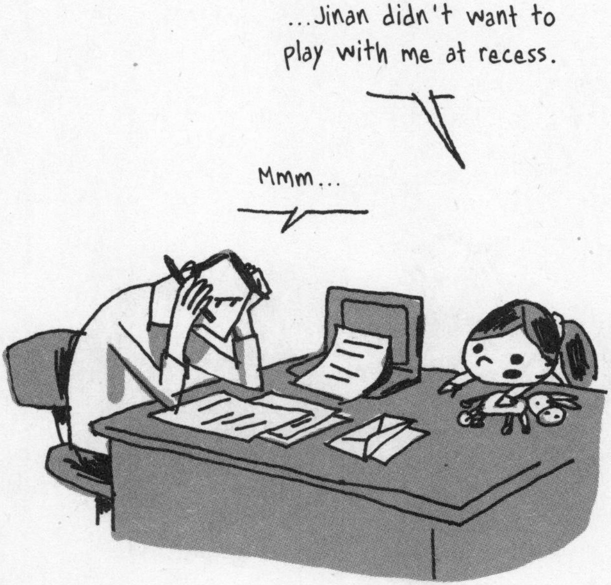
...Jinan didn't want to play with me at recess.
Mmm...

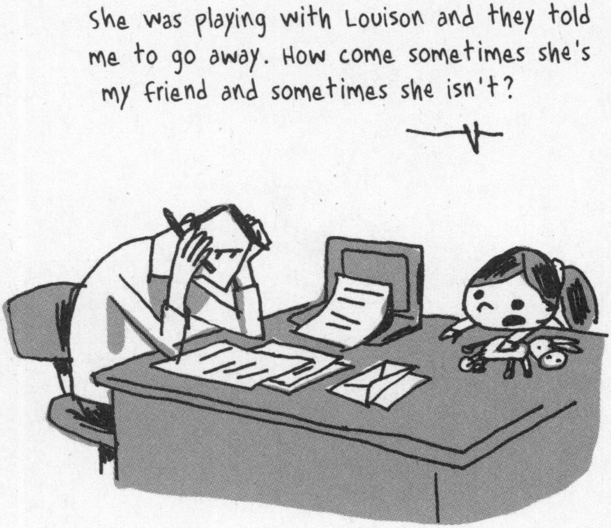
She was playing with Louison and they told me to go away. How come sometimes she's my friend and sometimes she isn't?

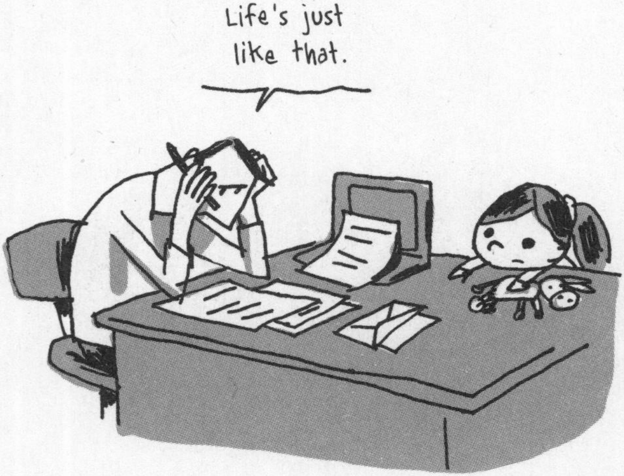
Life's just like that.

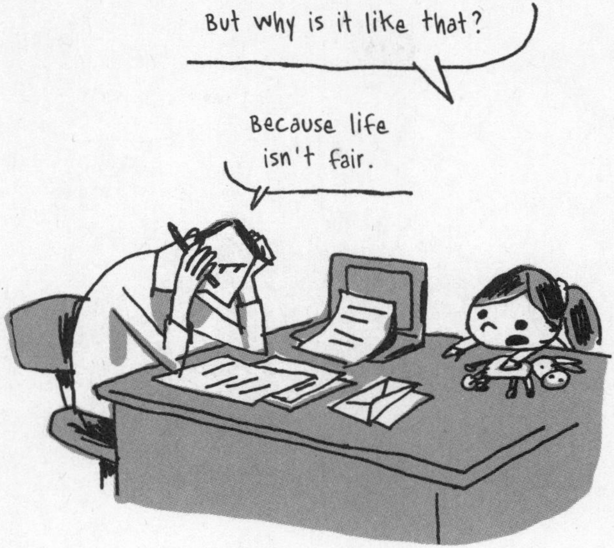
But why is it like that?
Because life isn't fair.

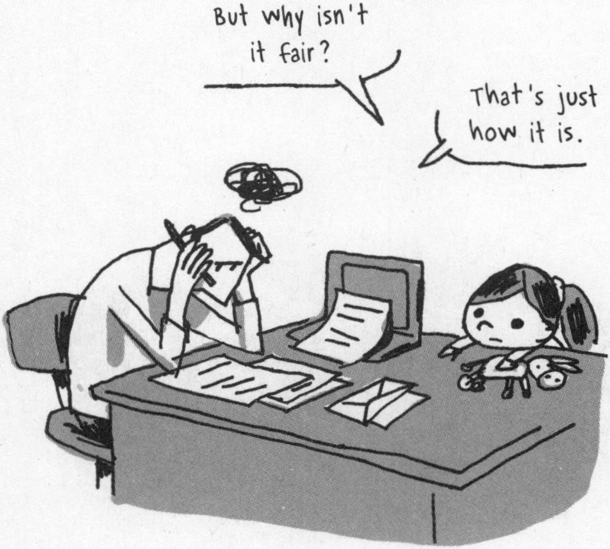
But why isn't it fair?
That's just how it is.

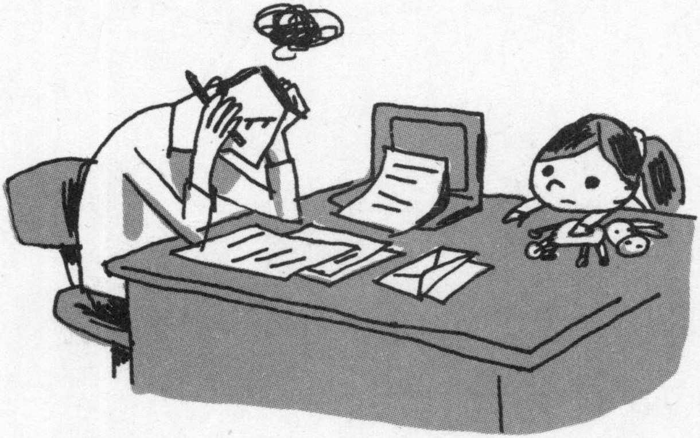

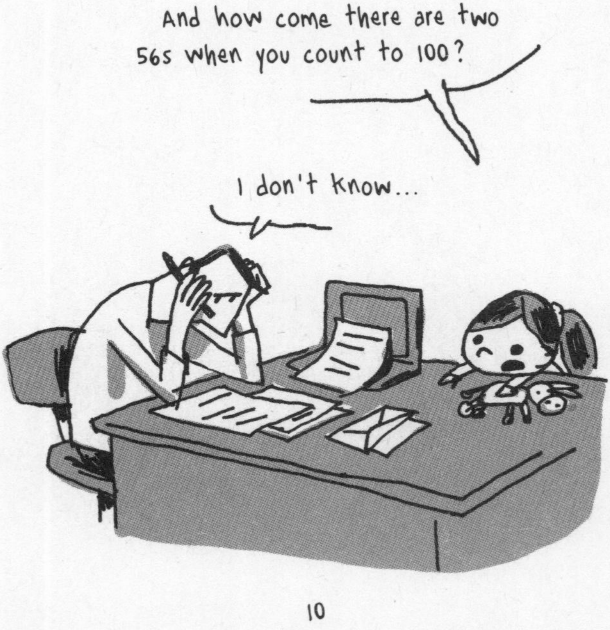
And how come there are two 56s when you count to 100?
I don't know...

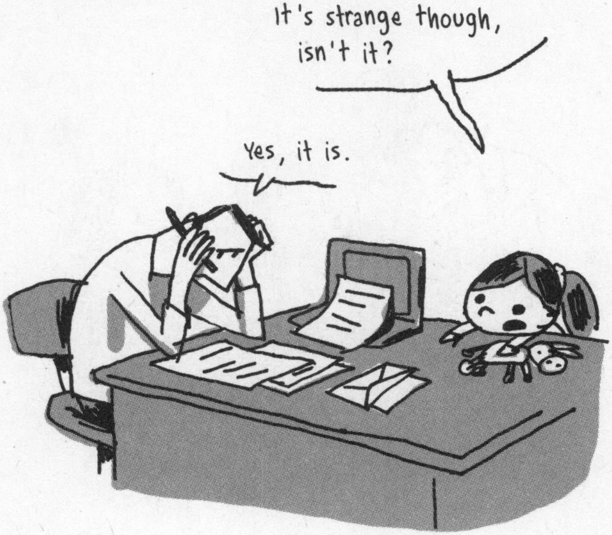
It's strange though, isn't it?
Yes, it is.

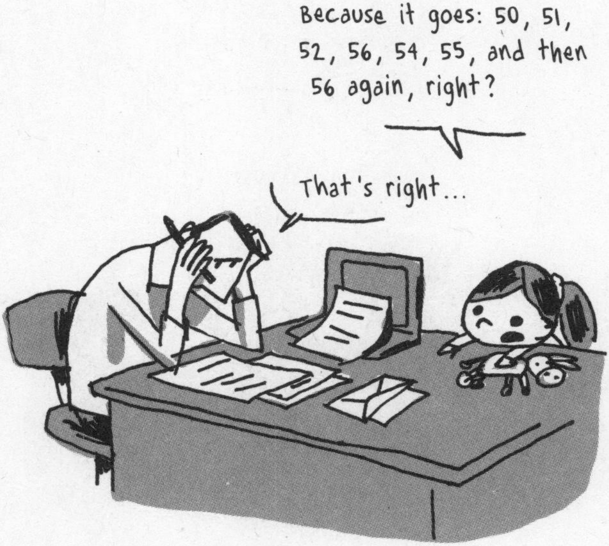
Because it goes: 50, 51, 52, 56, 54, 55, and then 56 again, right?
That's right...

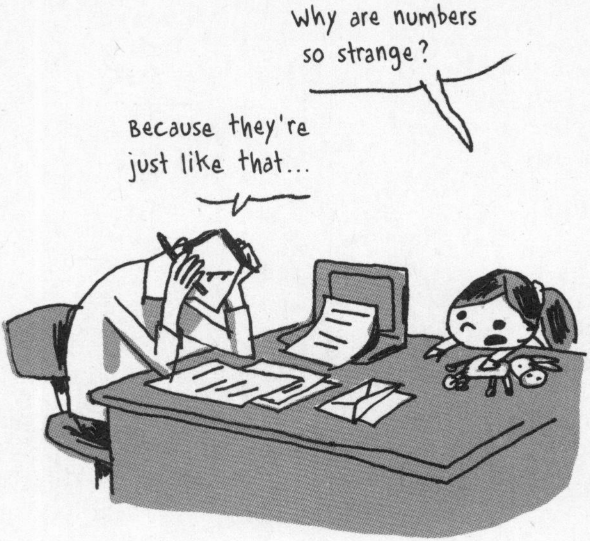
Why are numbers so strange?
Because they're just like that...

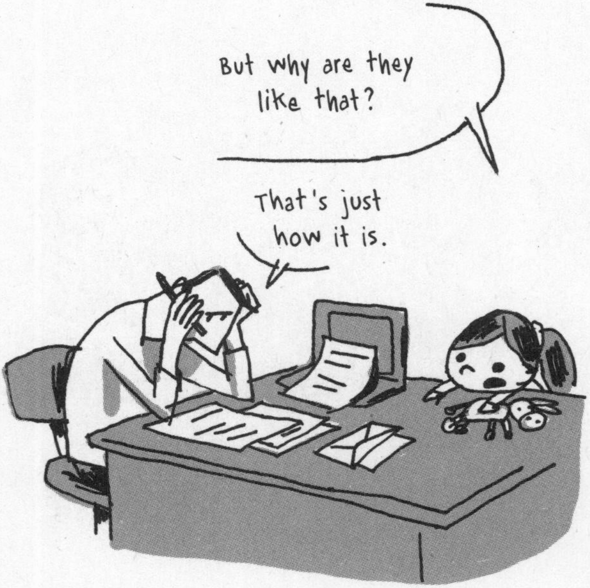
But why are they like that?
That's just how it is.

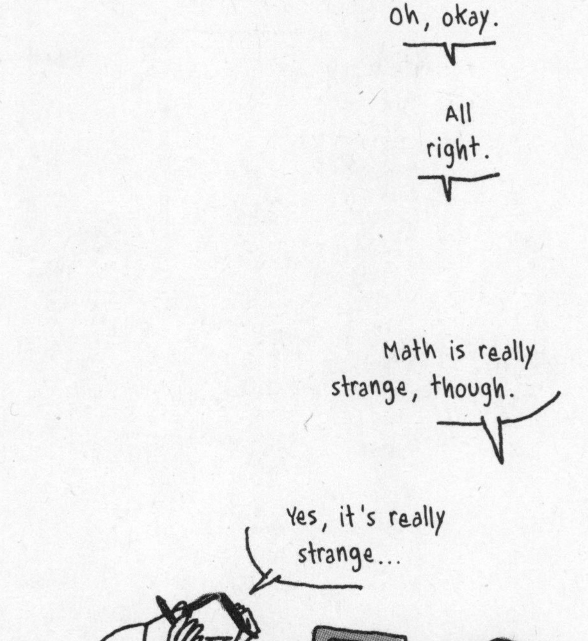
Oh, okay.
All right.
Math is really strange, though.
Yes, it's really strange...
DELISLE 2013

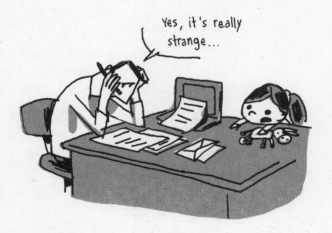

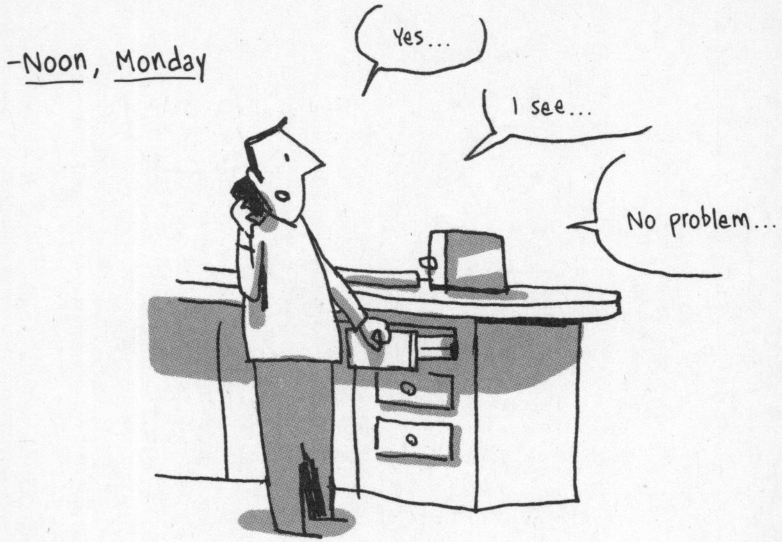
-Noon, Monday
Yes...
I see...
No problem...

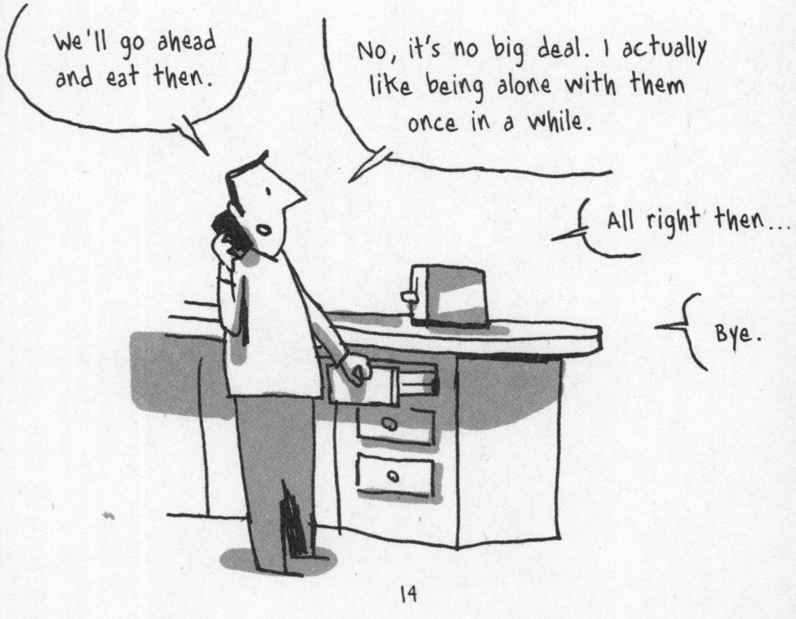
We'll go ahead and eat then.
No, it's no big deal. I actually like being alone with them once in a while.
All right then...
Bye.

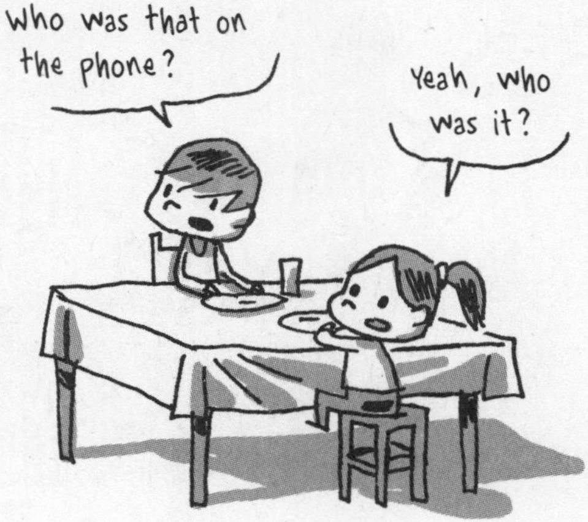
Who was that on the phone?
Yeah, who was it?

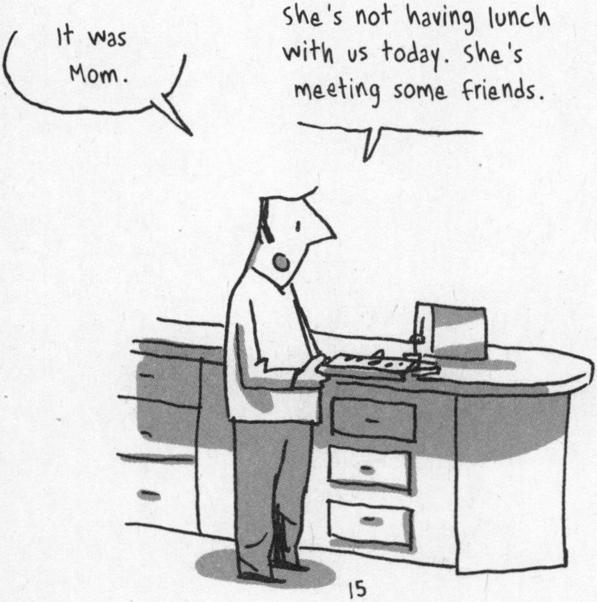
It was Mom.
She's not having lunch with us today. She's meeting some friends.

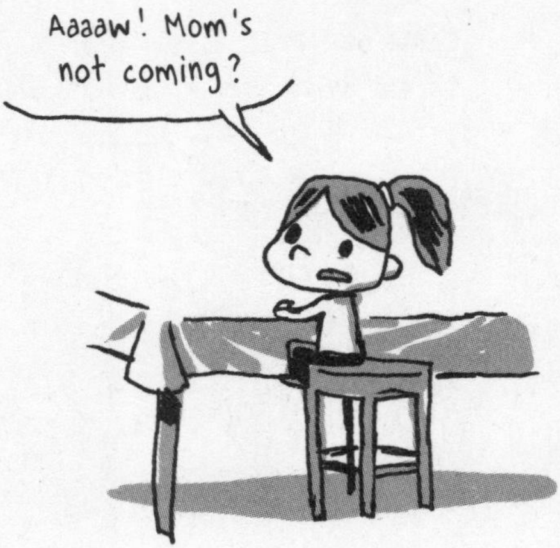
Aaaaw! Mom's not coming?

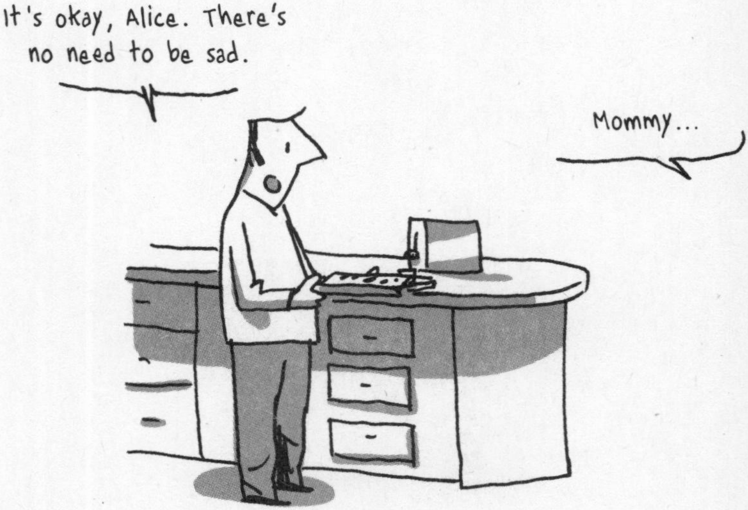
It's okay, Alice. There's no need to be sad.
Mommy...

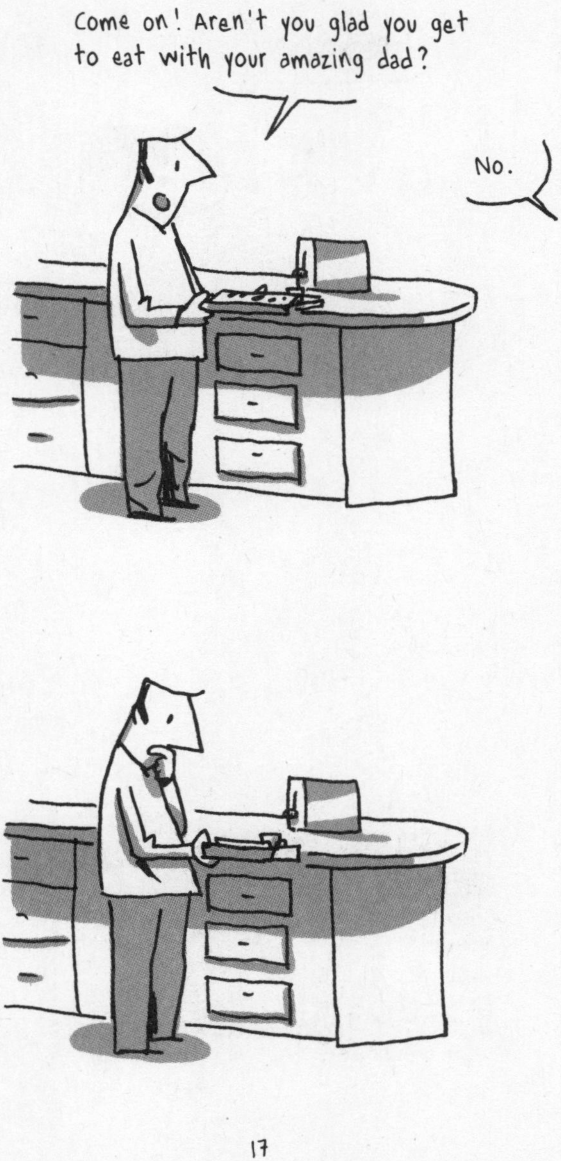
Come on! Aren't you glad you get to eat with your amazing dad?
No.

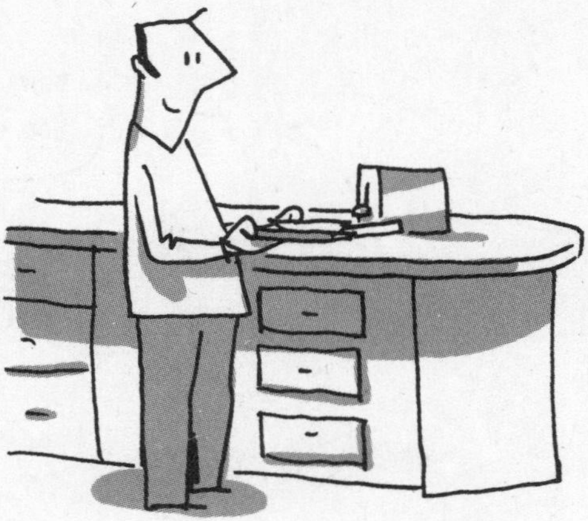

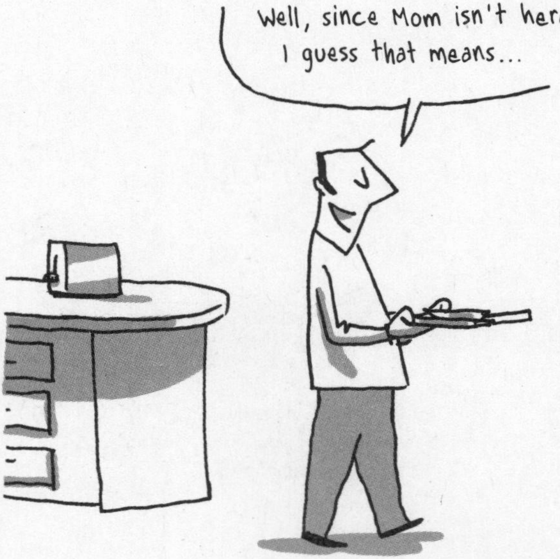
Well, since Mom isn't here, I guess that means...

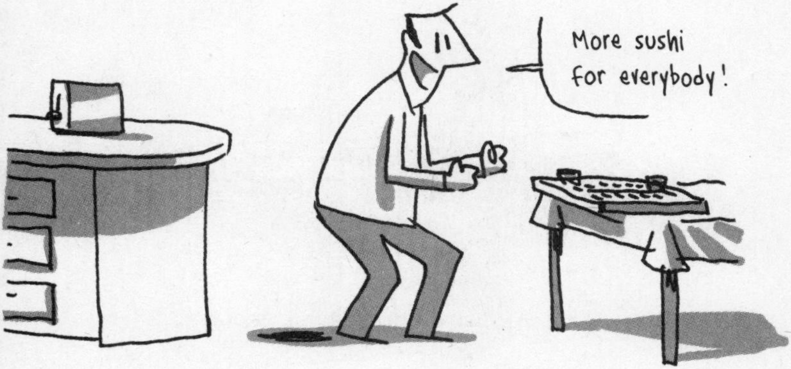
More sushi for everybody!

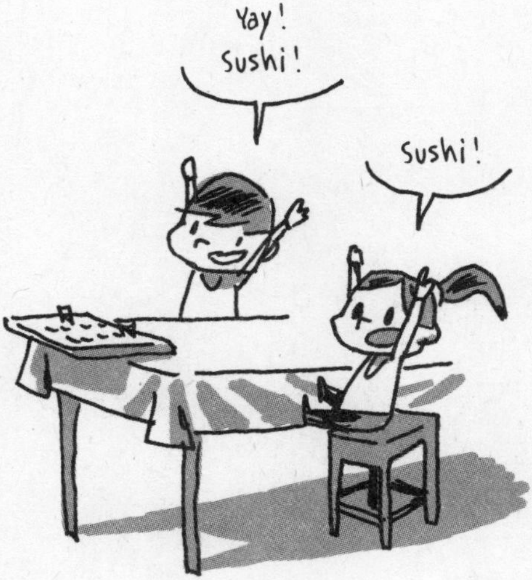
Yay! Sushi!
Sushi!

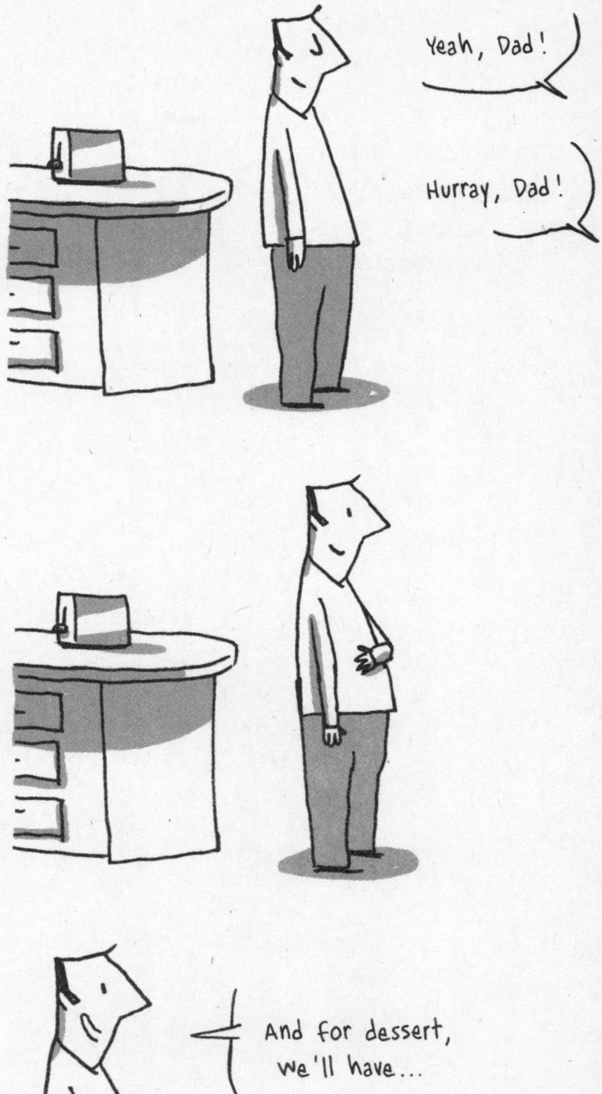
Yeah, Dad!
Hurray, Dad!
And for dessert, we'll have...

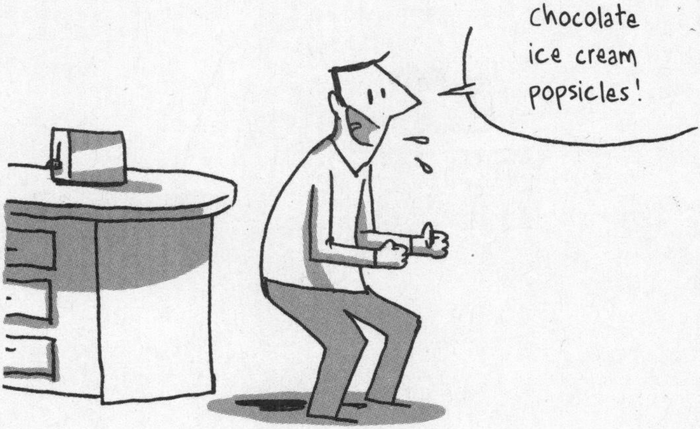
Chocolate ice cream popsicles!

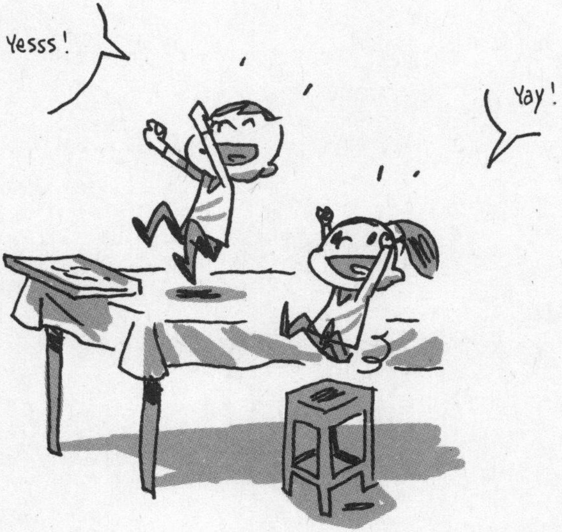
Yesss!
Yay!

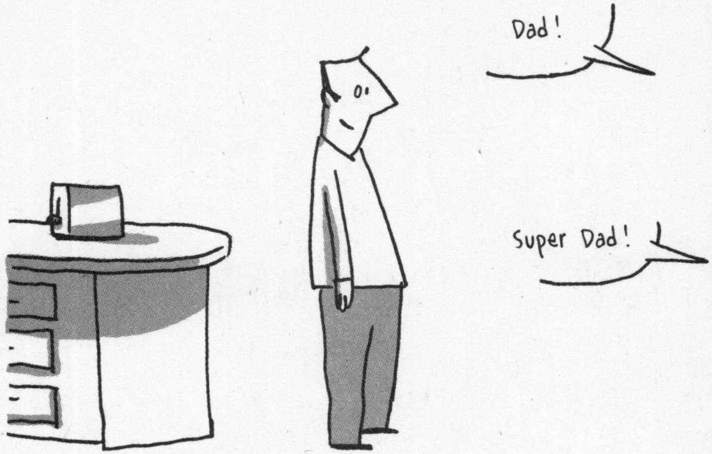
Dad!
Super Dad!

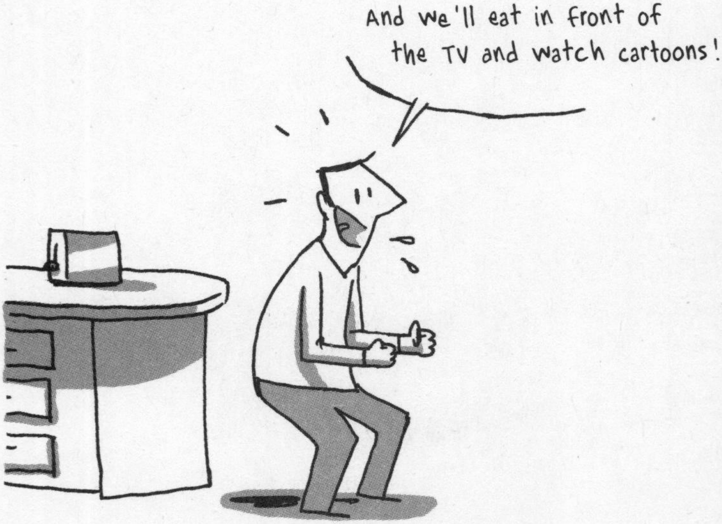
And we'll eat in front of the TV and watch cartoons!

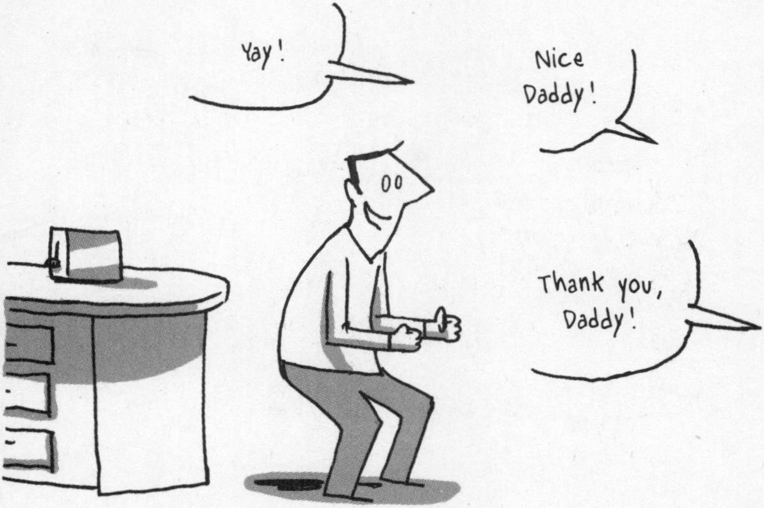
Yay!
Nice Daddy!
Thank you, Daddy!

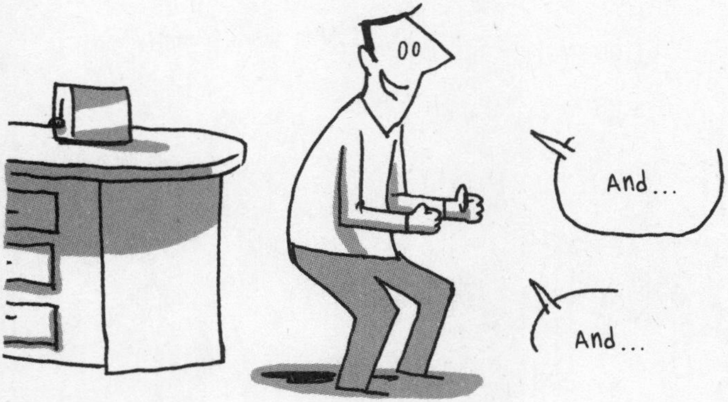
And...
And...

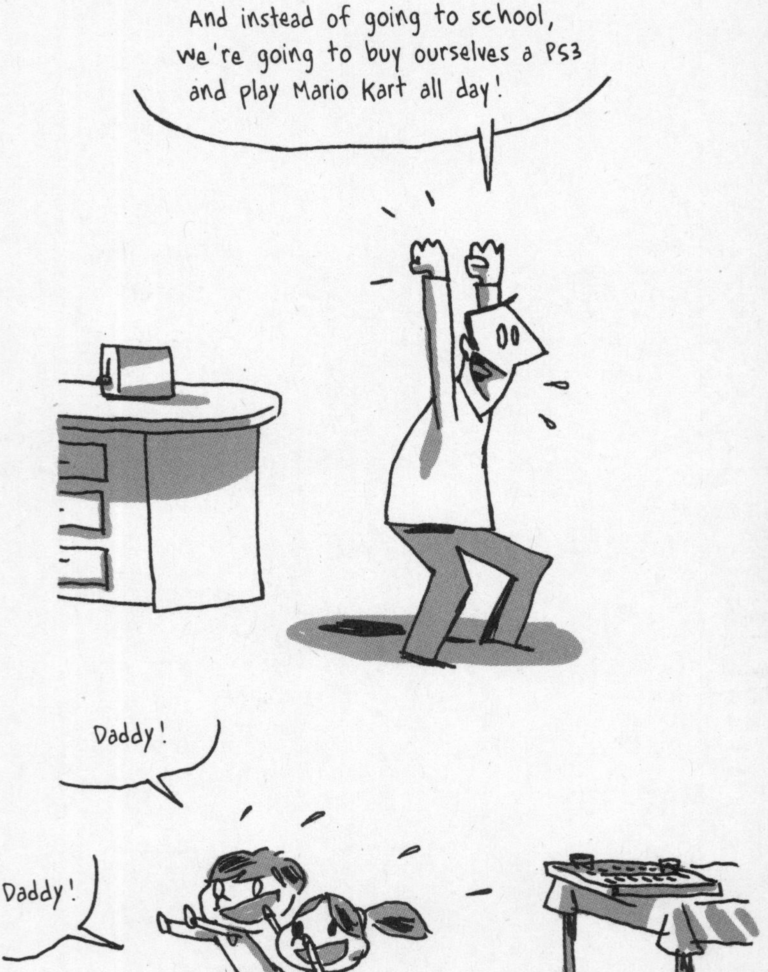
And instead of going to school, we're going to buy ourselves a PS3 and play Mario Kart all day!
Daddy!
Daddy!

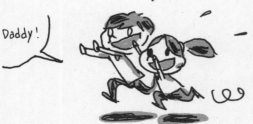

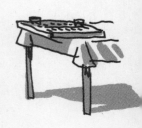

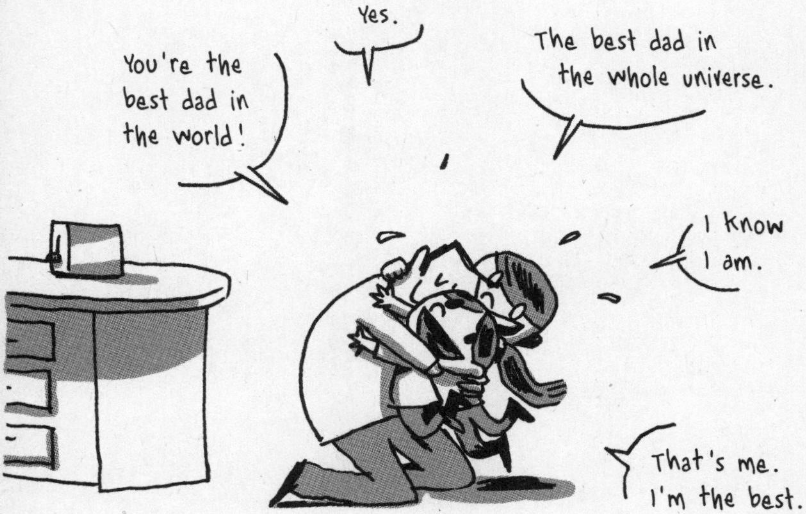
You're the best dad in the world!
Yes.
The best dad in the whole universe.
I know I am.
That's me. I'm the best.

DELISLE
2013

-Homework

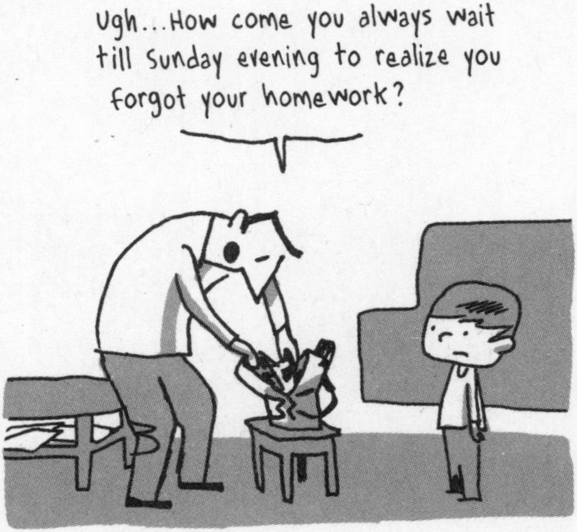
Ugh...How come you always wait till Sunday evening to realize you forgot your homework?

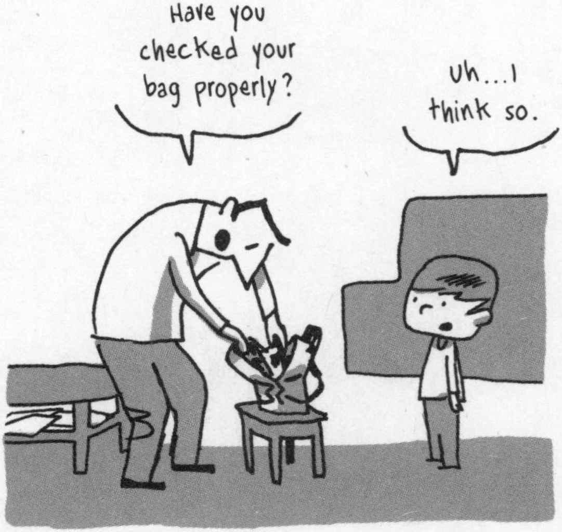
Have you checked your bag properly?
Uh...I think so.

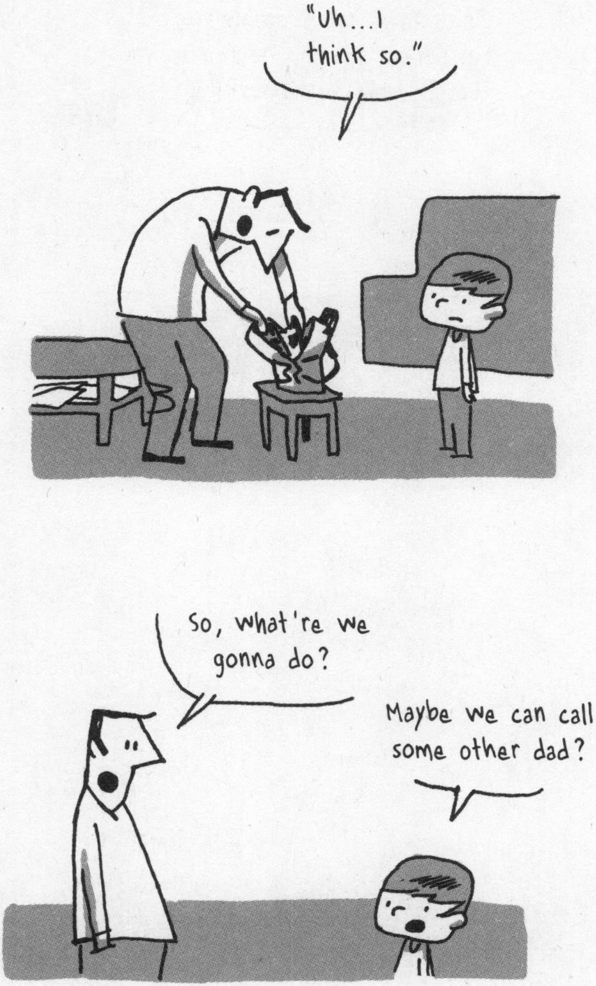
"Uh... I think so."
So, what're we gonna do?
Maybe we can call some other dad?

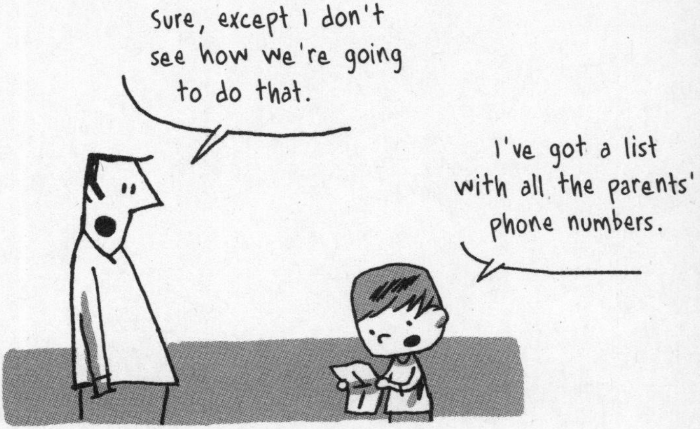
Sure, except I don't see how we're going to do that.
I've got a list with all the parents' phone numbers.

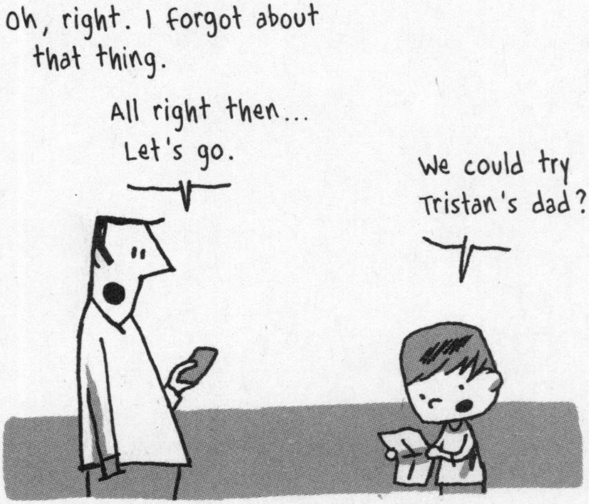
Oh, right. I forgot about that thing.
All right then... Let's go.
We could try Tristan's dad?

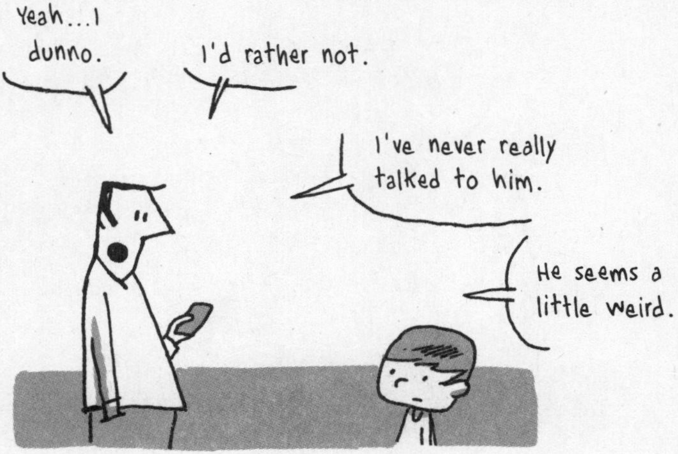
Yeah...I dunno.
I'd rather not.
I've never really talked to him.
He seems a little weird.

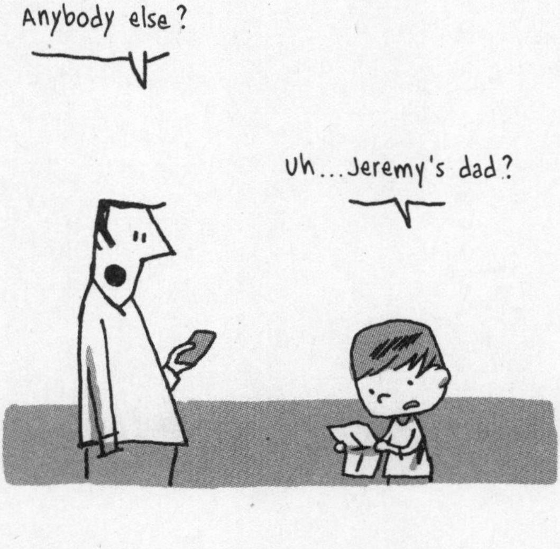
Anybody else?
Uh...Jeremy's dad?

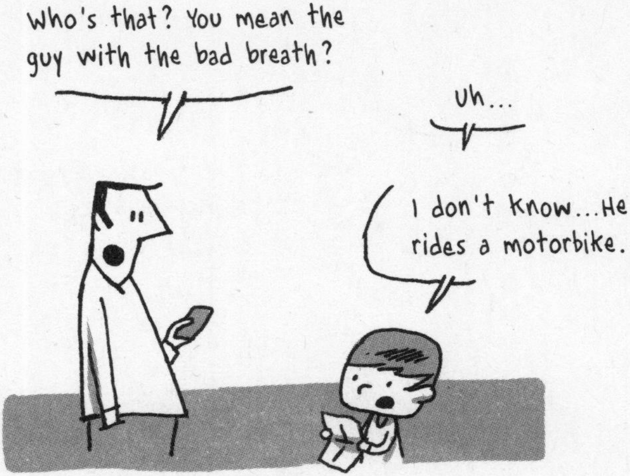
Who's that? You mean the guy with the bad breath?
Uh...
I don't know...He rides a motorbike.

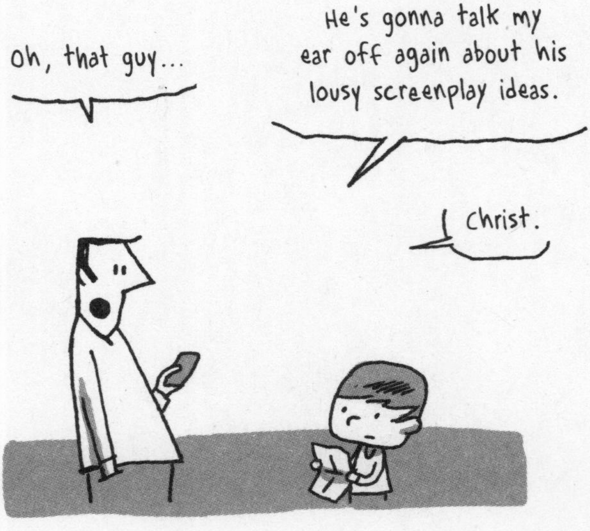
Oh, that guy...
He's gonna talk my ear off again about his lousy screenplay ideas.
Christ.

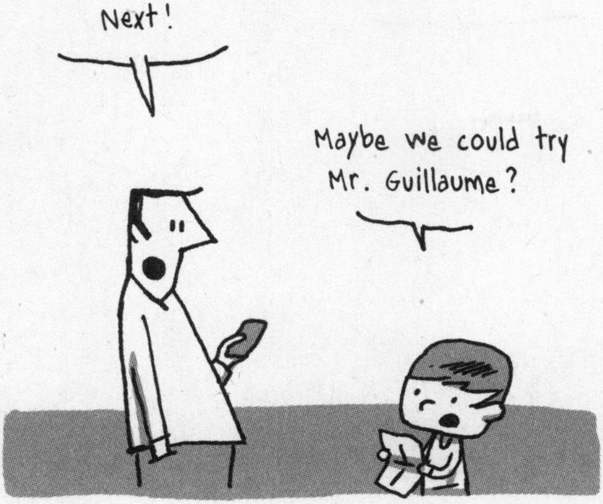
Next!
Maybe we could try Mr. Guillaume?

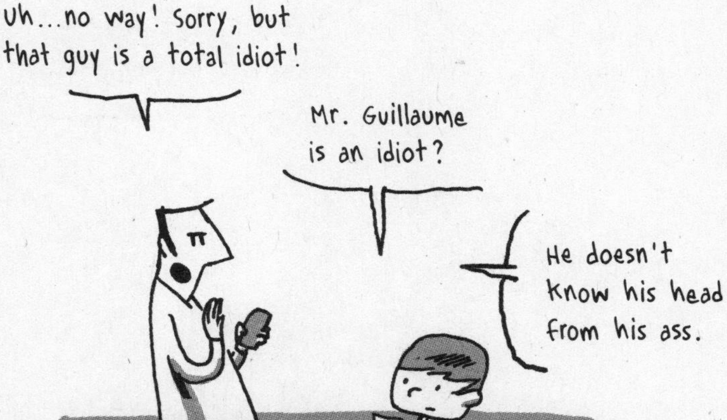
Uh...no way! Sorry, but that guy is a total idiot!
Mr. Guillaume is an idiot?
He doesn't know his head from his ass.

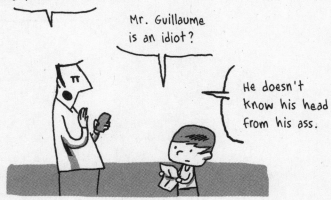

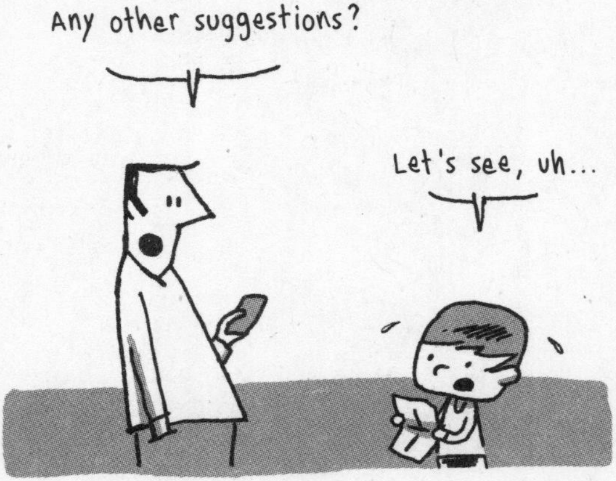
Any other suggestions?
Let's see, uh...

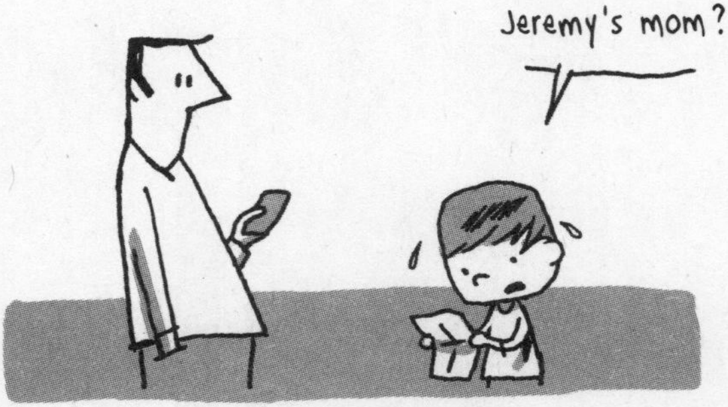
Jeremy's mom?

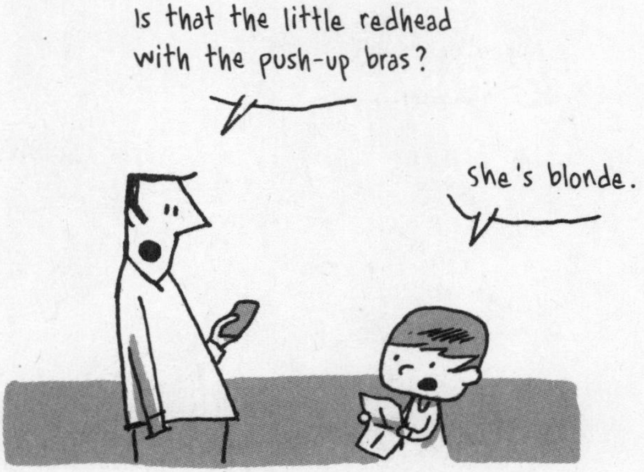
Is that the little redhead with the push-up bras?
She's blonde.

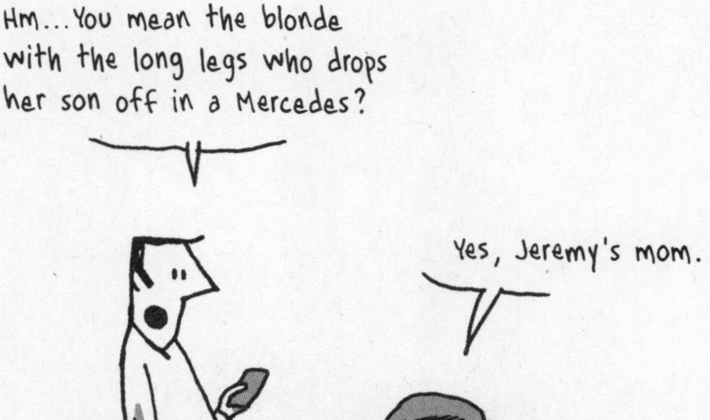
Hm... You mean the blonde with the long legs who drops her son off in a Mercedes?
Yes, Jeremy's mom.

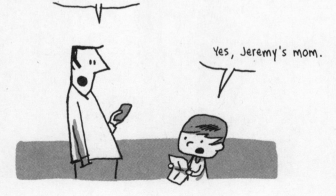

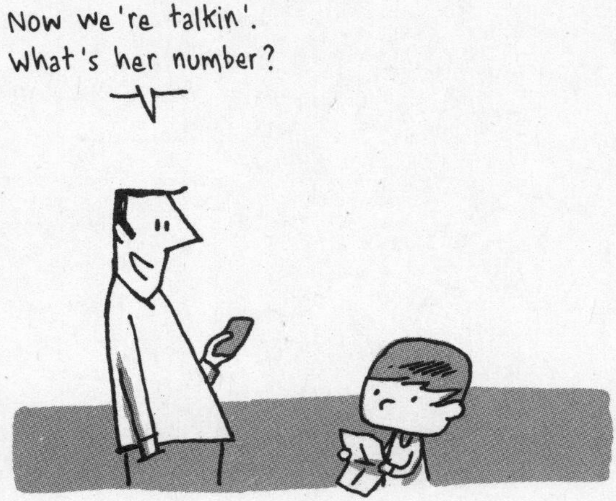
Now we're talkin'. What's her number?

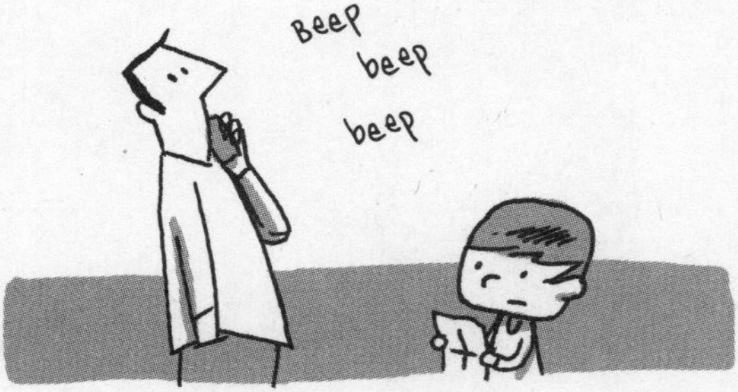
Beep
beep
beep

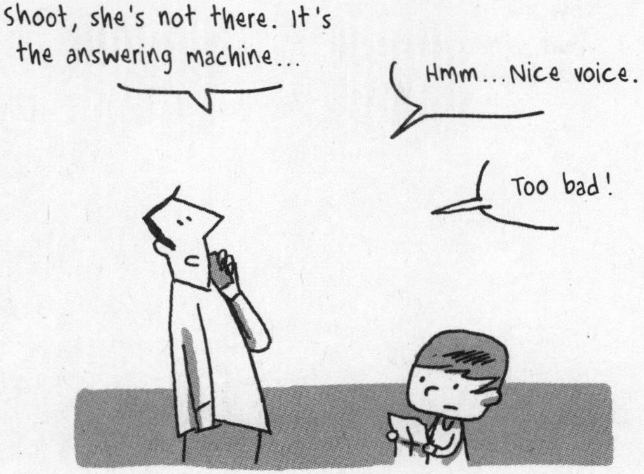
Shoot, she's not there. It's the answering machine...
Hmm...Nice voice.
Too bad!

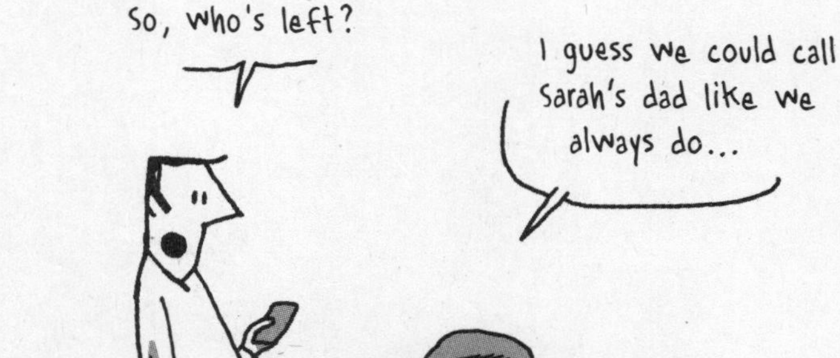
So, who's left?
I guess we could call Sarah's dad like we always do...

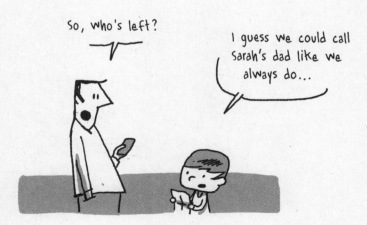

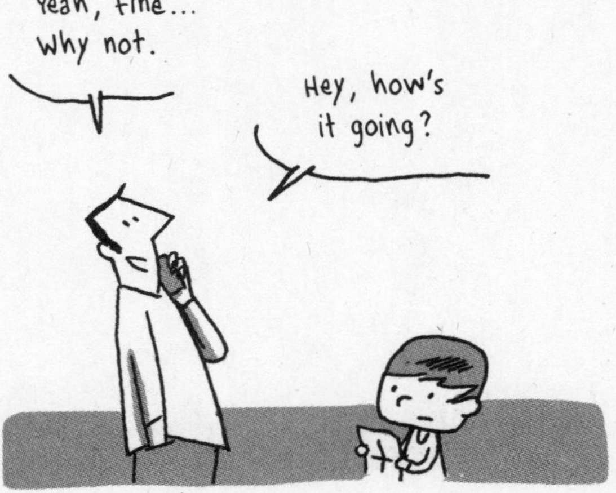
Yeah, fine... Why not.
Hey, how's it going?

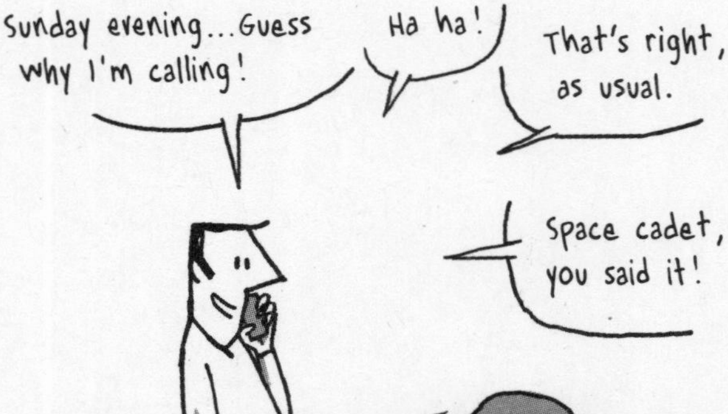
Sunday evening... Guess why I'm calling!
Ha ha!
That's right, as usual.
Space cadet, you said it!

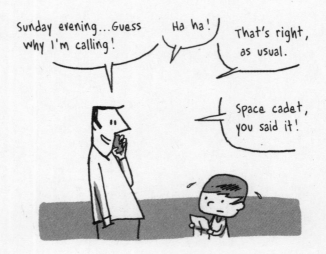

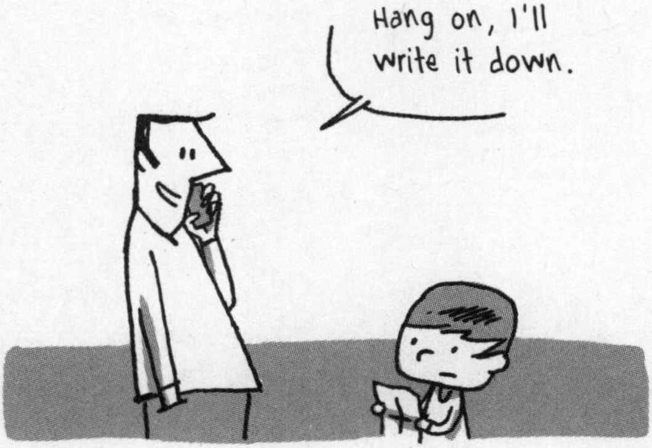
Hang on, I'll write it down.

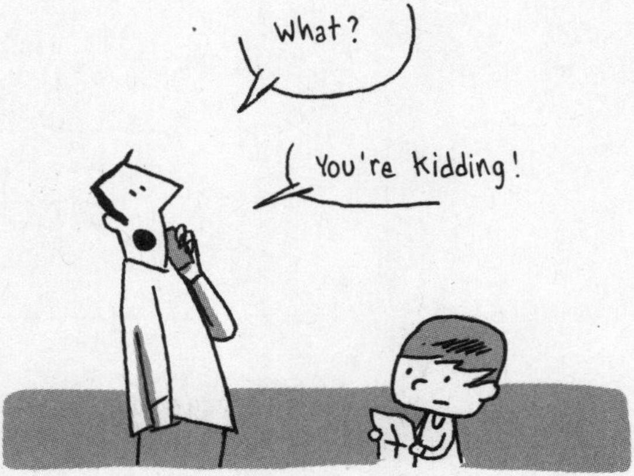
What?
You're kidding!

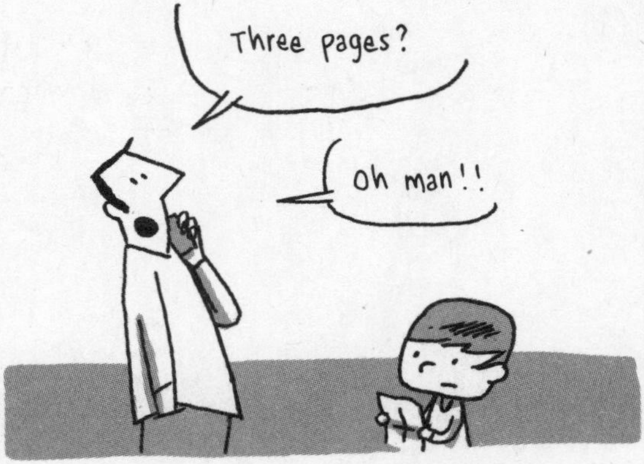
Three pages?
Oh man!!

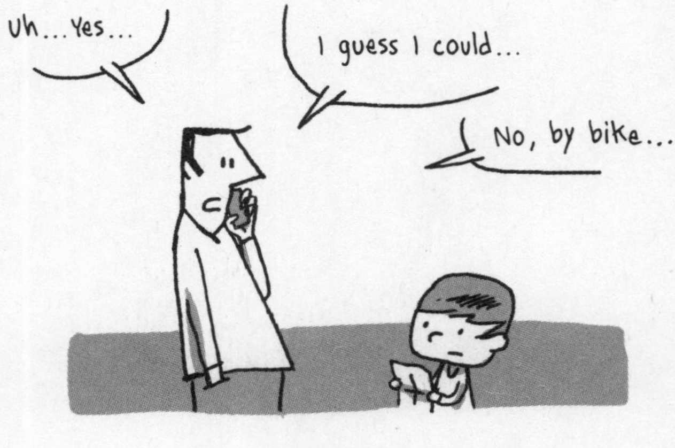
Uh... Yes...
I guess I could...
No, by bike...

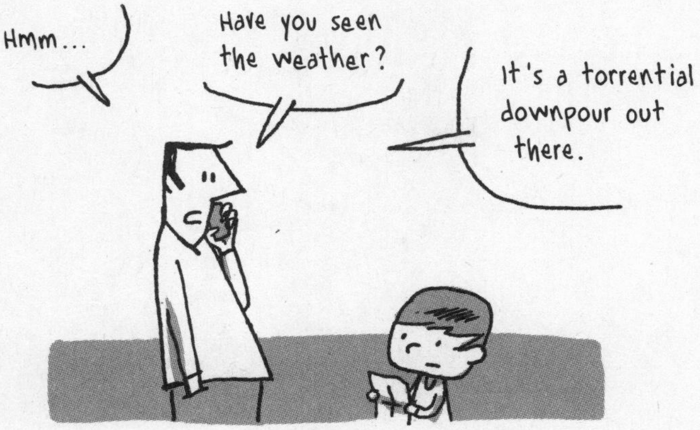
Hmm...
Have you seen the weather?
It's a torrential downpour out there.

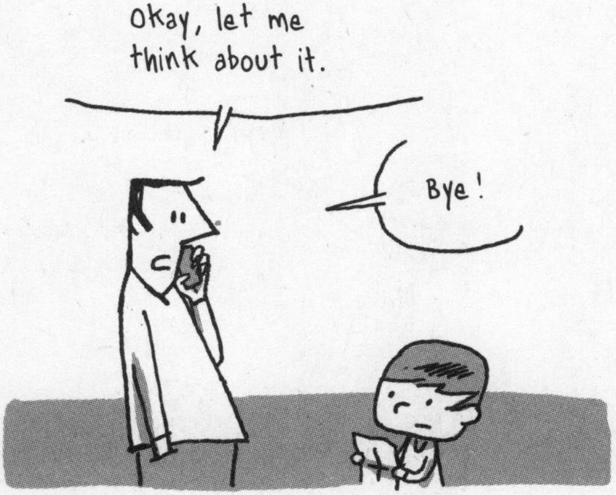
Okay, let me think about it.
Bye!

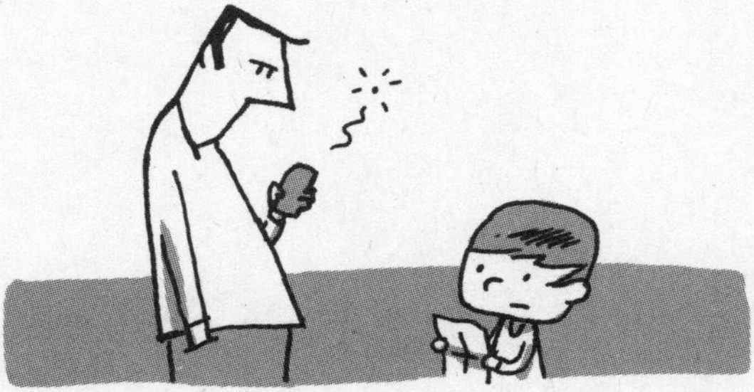

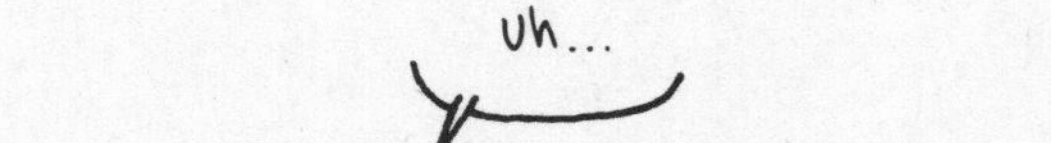
uh...

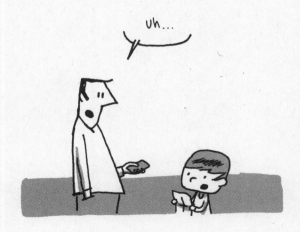

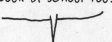

No go. His daughter left her book at school too.

DELISLE
2013

-The Visitor

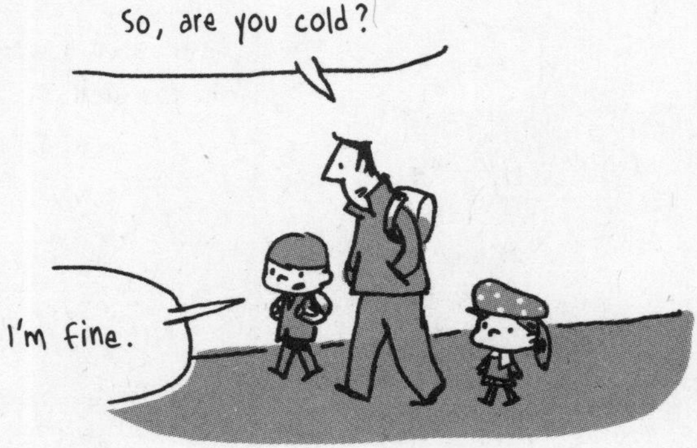
So, are you cold?
I'm fine.

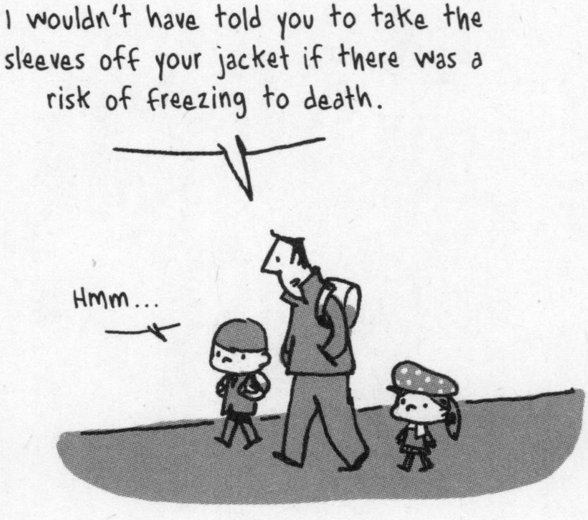
I wouldn't have told you to take the sleeves off your jacket if there was a risk of freezing to death.
Hmm...

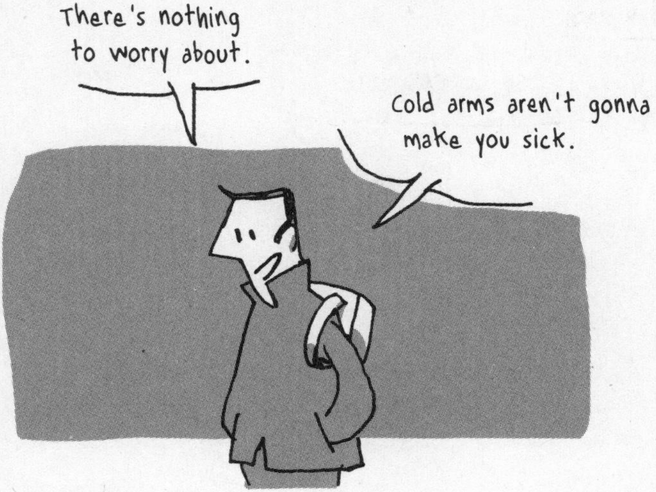
There's nothing to worry about.
Cold arms aren't gonna make you sick.

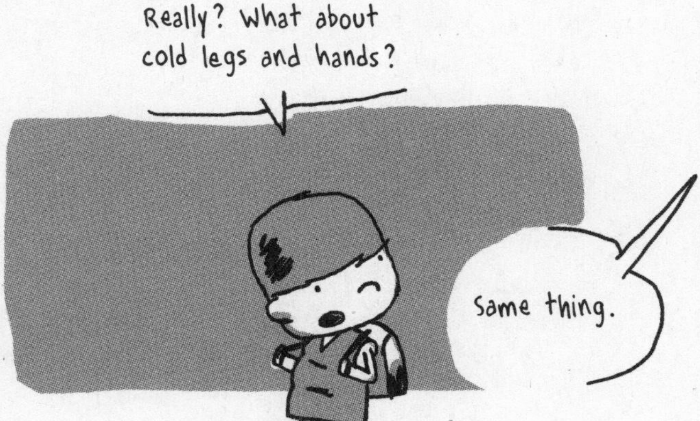
Really? What about cold legs and hands?
Same thing.

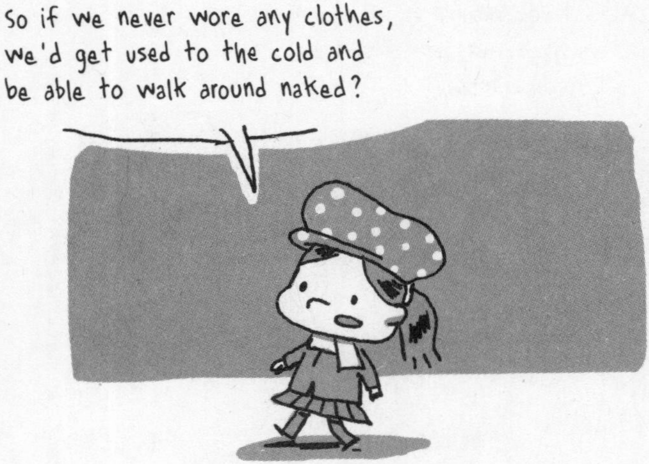
So if we never wore any clothes, we'd get used to the cold and be able to walk around naked?

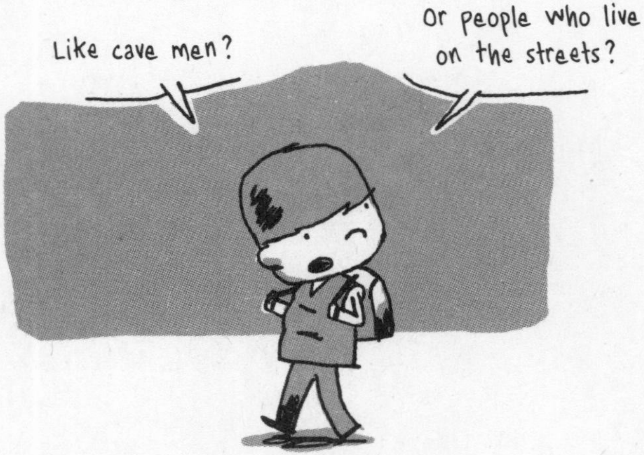
Like cave men?
Or people who live on the streets?

It's true. People who live on the streets are able to sleep in the snow.

Uh...they do become pretty resistant to the cold, but when it snows, they go to shelters.

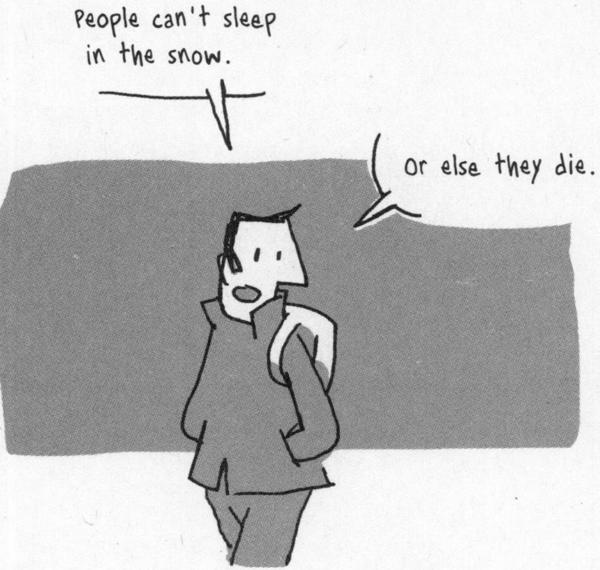
People can't sleep in the snow.
Or else they die.

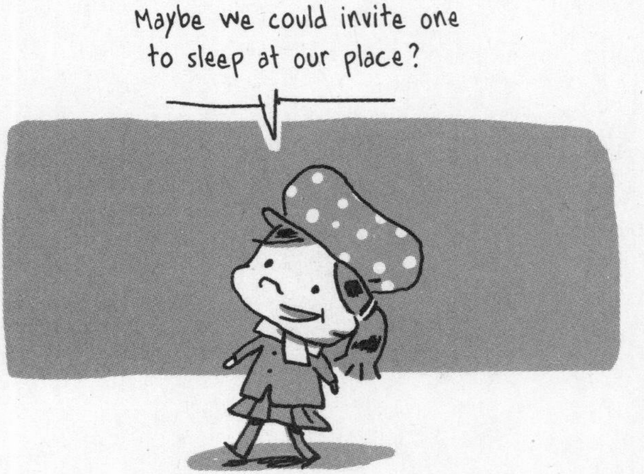
Maybe we could invite one to sleep at our place?

Sure, great idea.
Sound good, Louis?

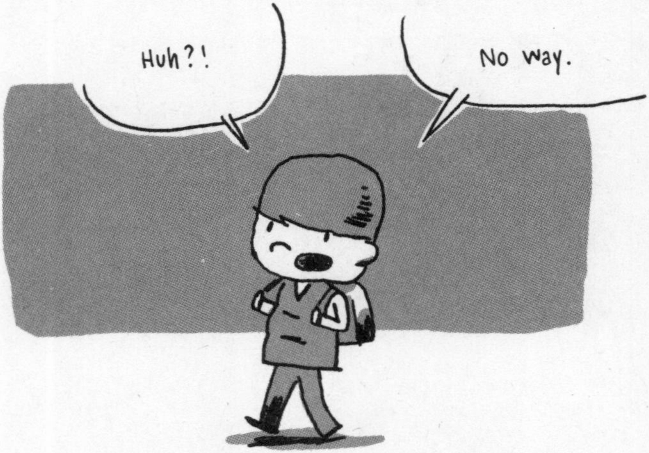
Huh?!
No way.

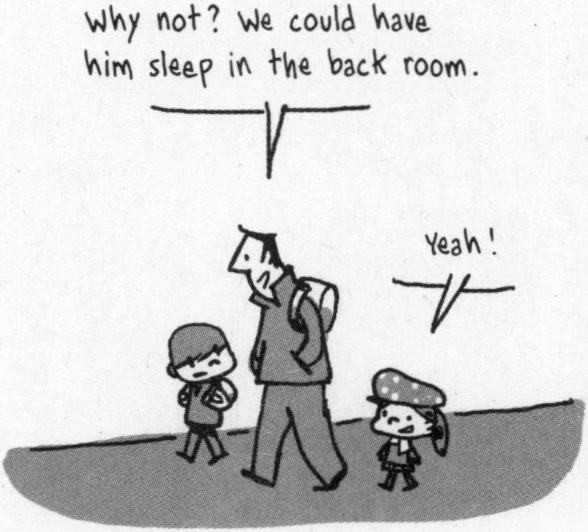
Why not? We could have him sleep in the back room.
Yeah!

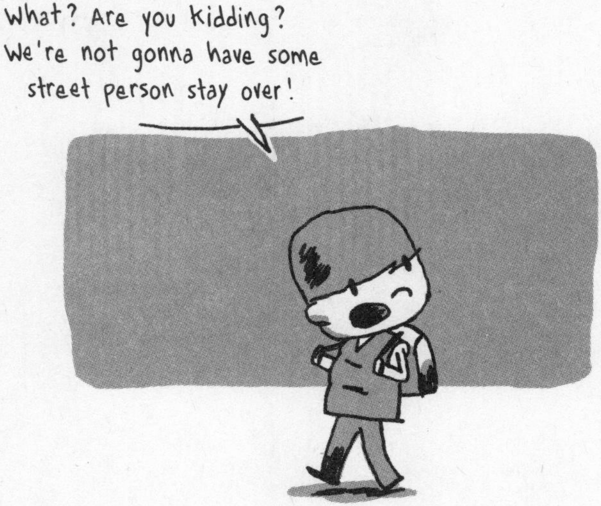
What? Are you kidding? We're not gonna have some street person stay over!

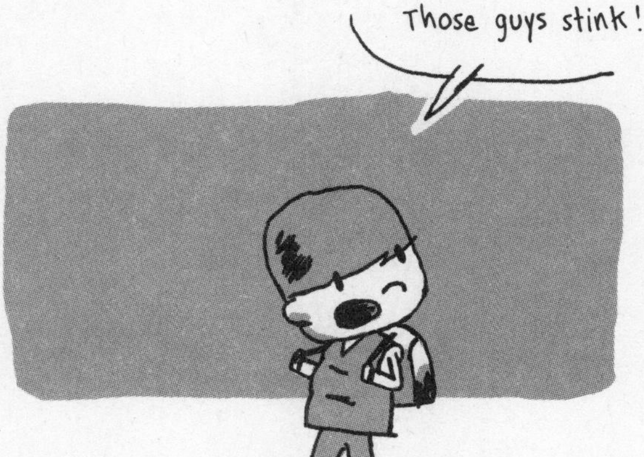
Those guys stink!

He could take a bath.

Yeah!

We'd need to feed him, too.
I hope he won't eat all the
chocolate cookies we baked
with Alice.

Huh, Alice?

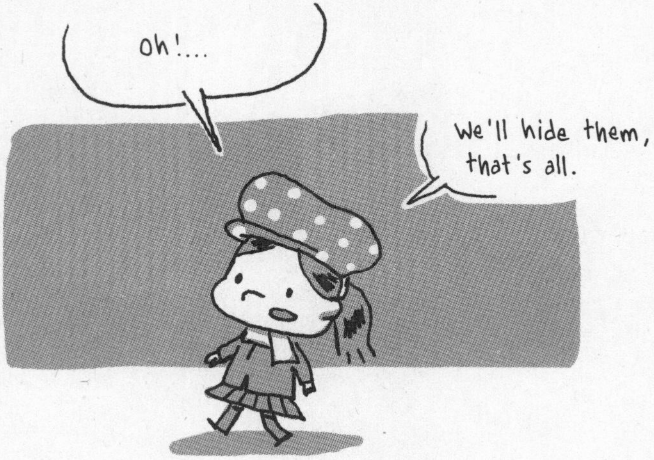
Oh!...
We'll hide them, that's all.

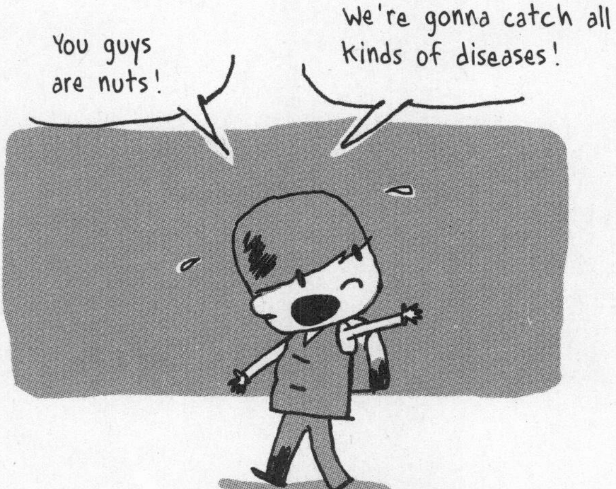
We're gonna catch all kinds of diseases!
You guys are nuts!

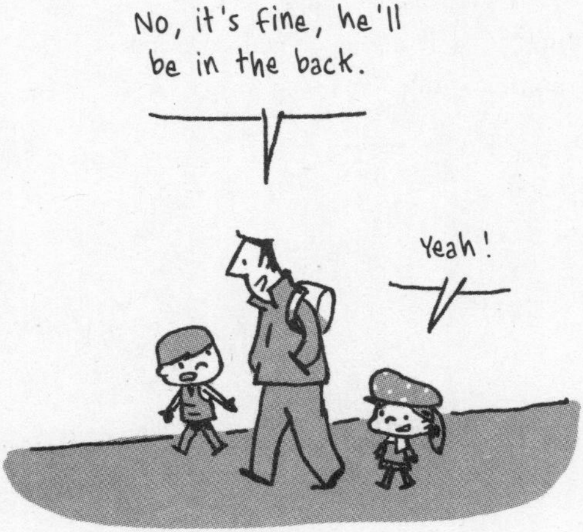
No, it's fine, he'll be in the back.
Yeah!

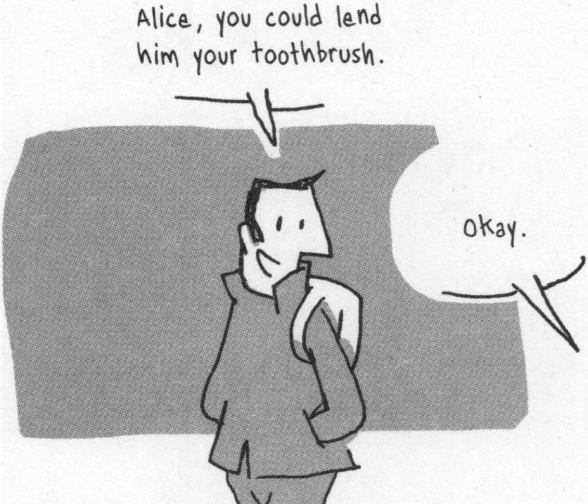
Alice, you could lend him your toothbrush.
Okay.

And if he needs something at night, he'll come knock on your door, seeing that we're upstairs.

Perfect.

Actually, Alice, maybe you could give him your bed? That way you can sleep in the living room and keep an eye on your chocolate cookies.

Oh, yeah! Good idea!

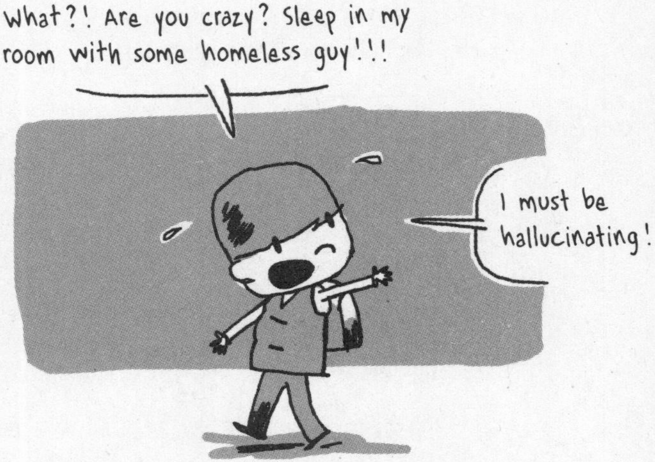
What?! Are you crazy? Sleep in my room with some homeless guy!!!
I must be hallucinating!

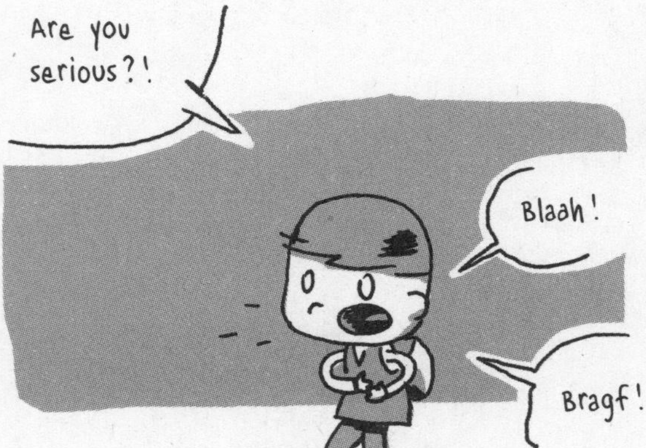
Are you serious?!
Blaah!
Bragf!

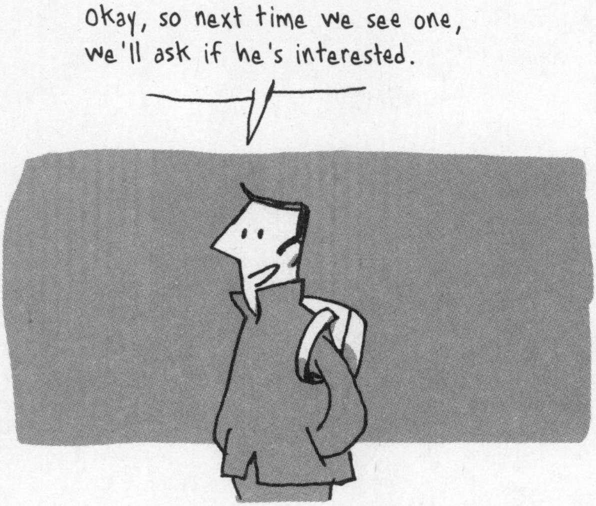
Okay, so next time we see one, we'll ask if he's interested.

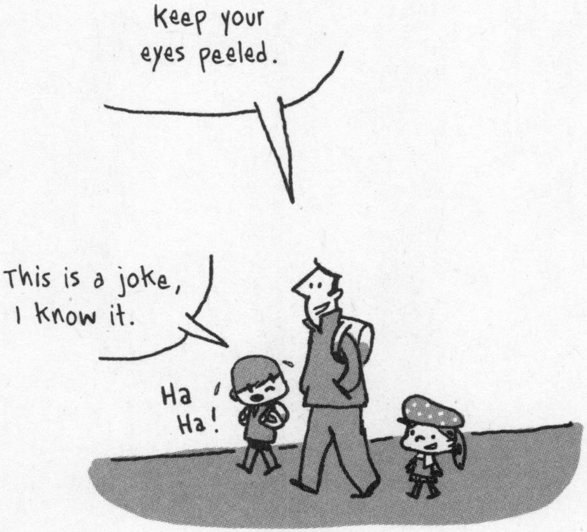
Keep your eyes peeled.
This is a joke, I know it.
Ha! Ha!

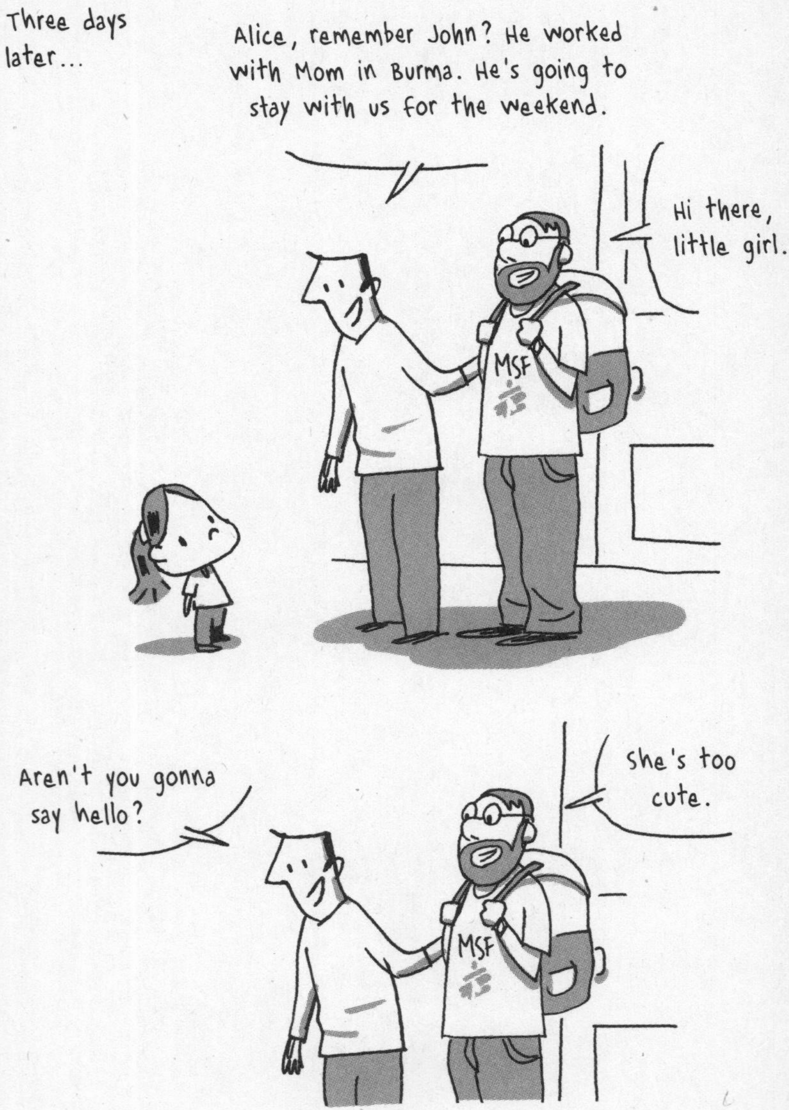
Three days later...
Alice, remember John? He worked with Mom in Burma. He's going to stay with us for the weekend.
Hi there, little girl.
Aren't you gonna say hello?
She's too cute.
MSF
MSF

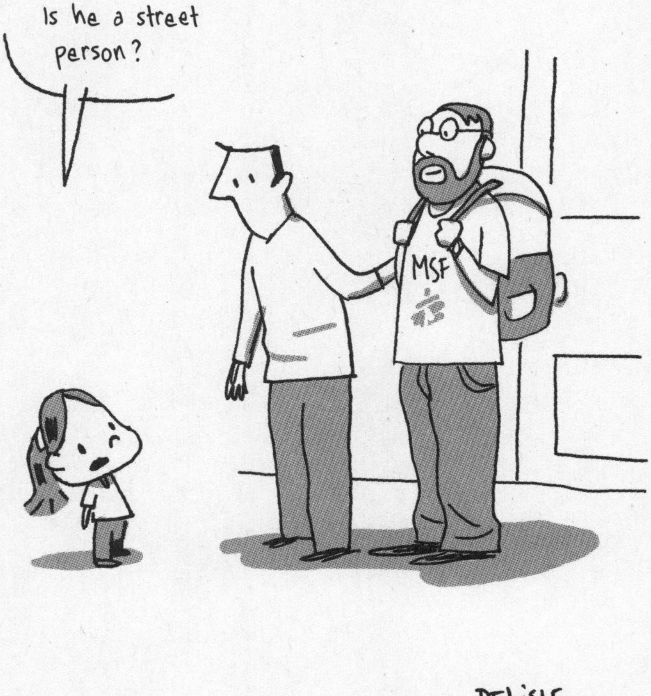
Is he a street person?
MSF
DELISLE 2013

-The Tooth

So, how's that tooth?
Finally out?

Not yet.

Look!

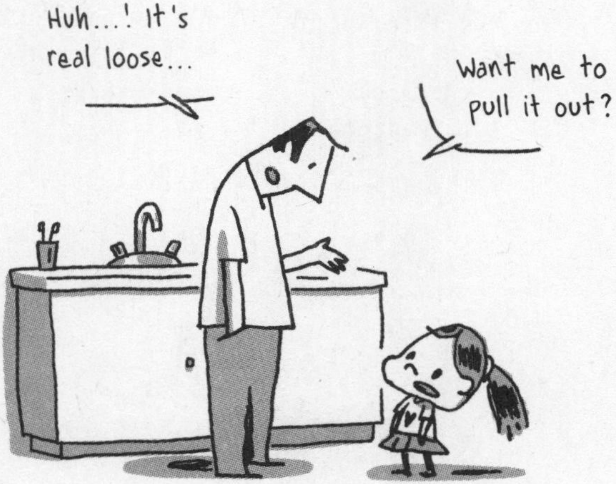
Huh...! It's real loose...
Want me to pull it out?

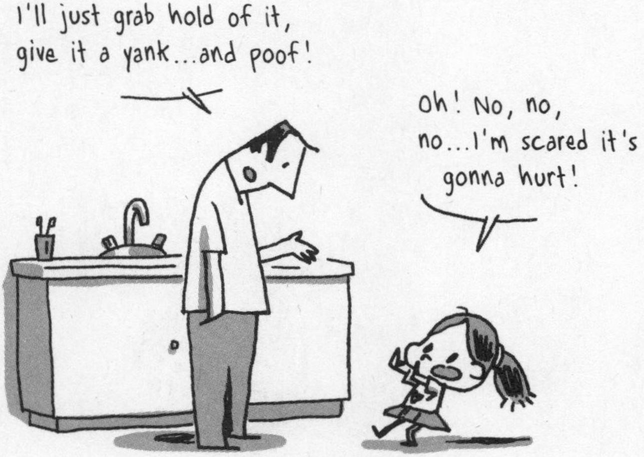
I'll just grab hold of it, give it a yank...and poof!
Oh! No, no, no...I'm scared it's gonna hurt!

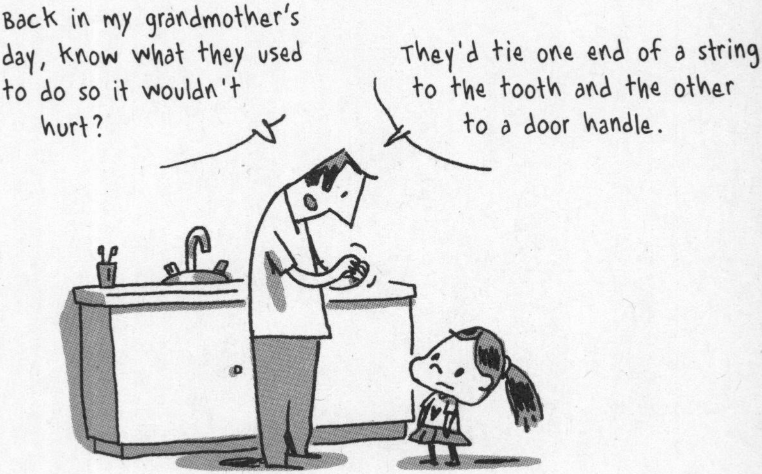
Back in my grandmother's day, know what they used to do so it wouldn't hurt?
They'd tie one end of a string to the tooth and the other to a door handle.
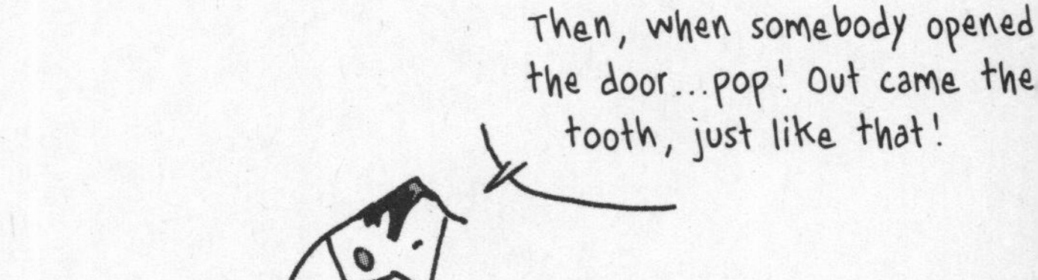
Then, when somebody opened the door...pop! Out came the tooth, just like that!
Oh!

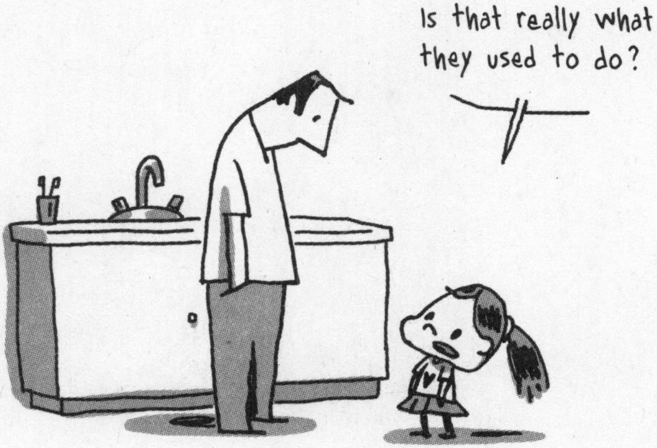
Is that really what they used to do?

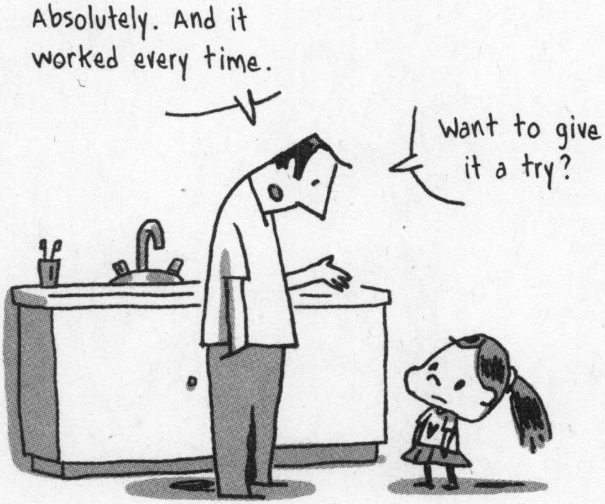
Absolutely. And it worked every time.
Want to give it a try?

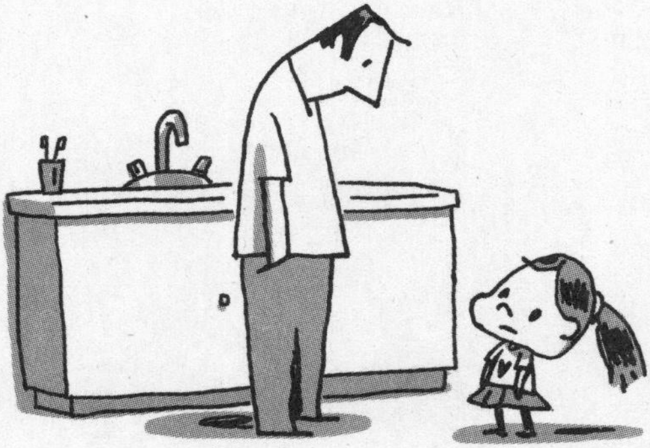

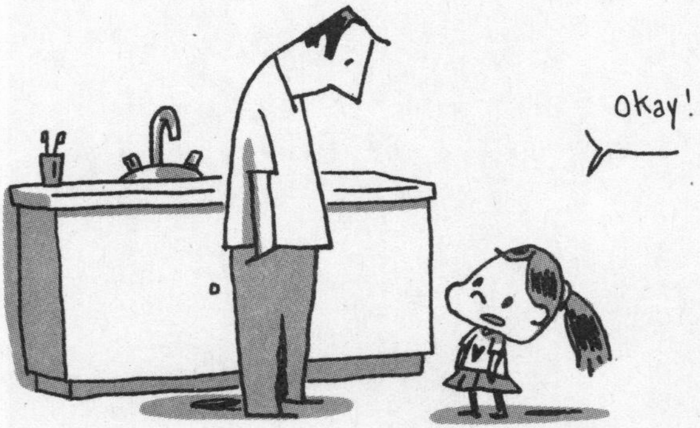
Okay!

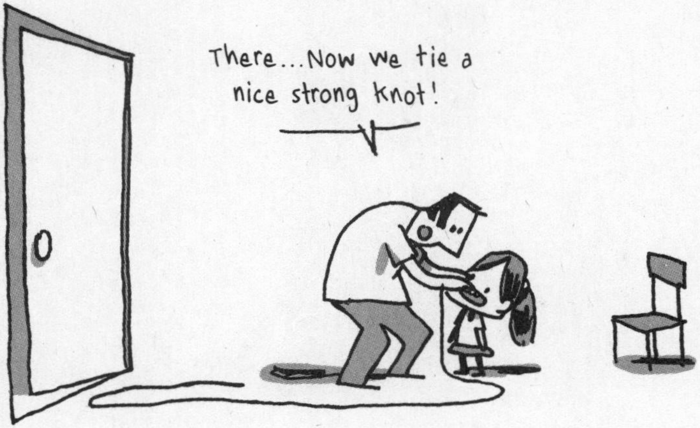
There... Now we tie a nice strong knot!

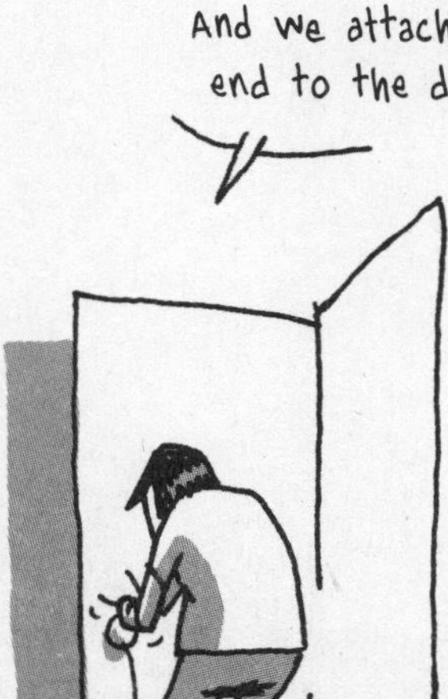
And we attach the other end to the door handle.

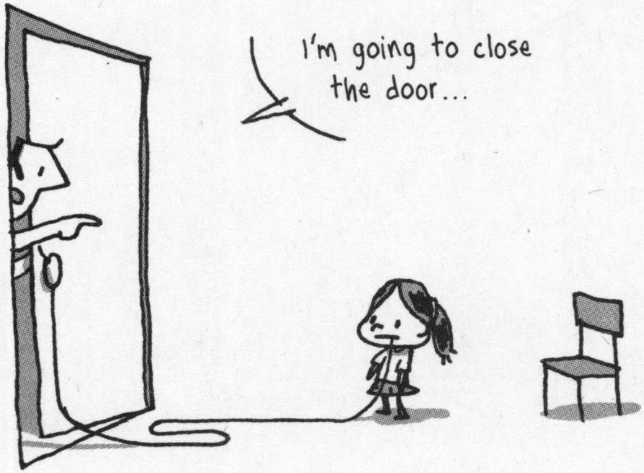
I'm going to close the door...

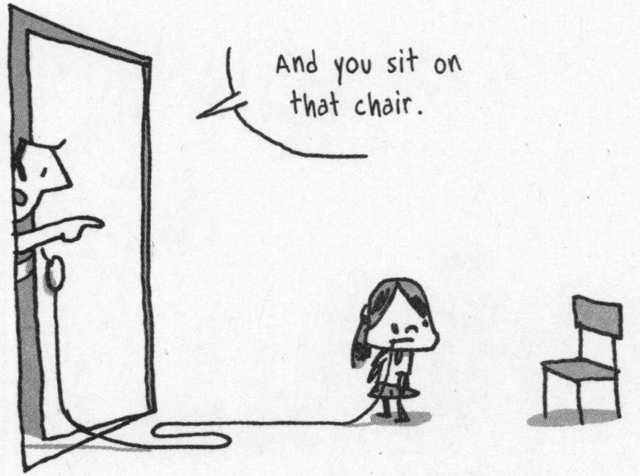
And you sit on that chair.

C'mon, get moving!

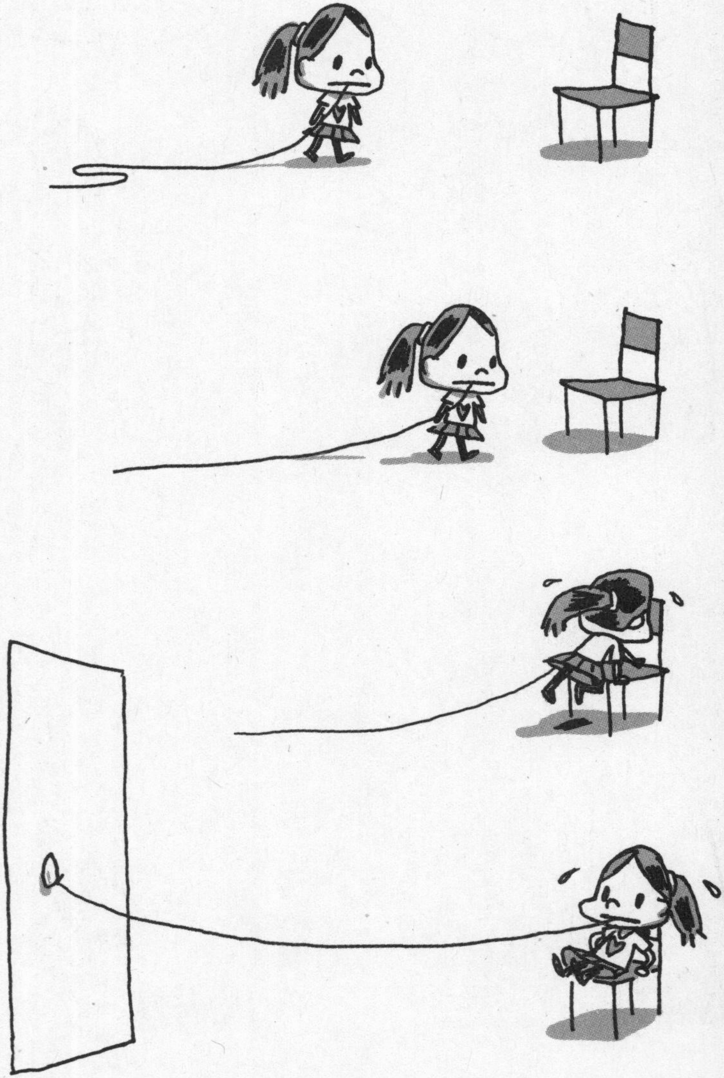

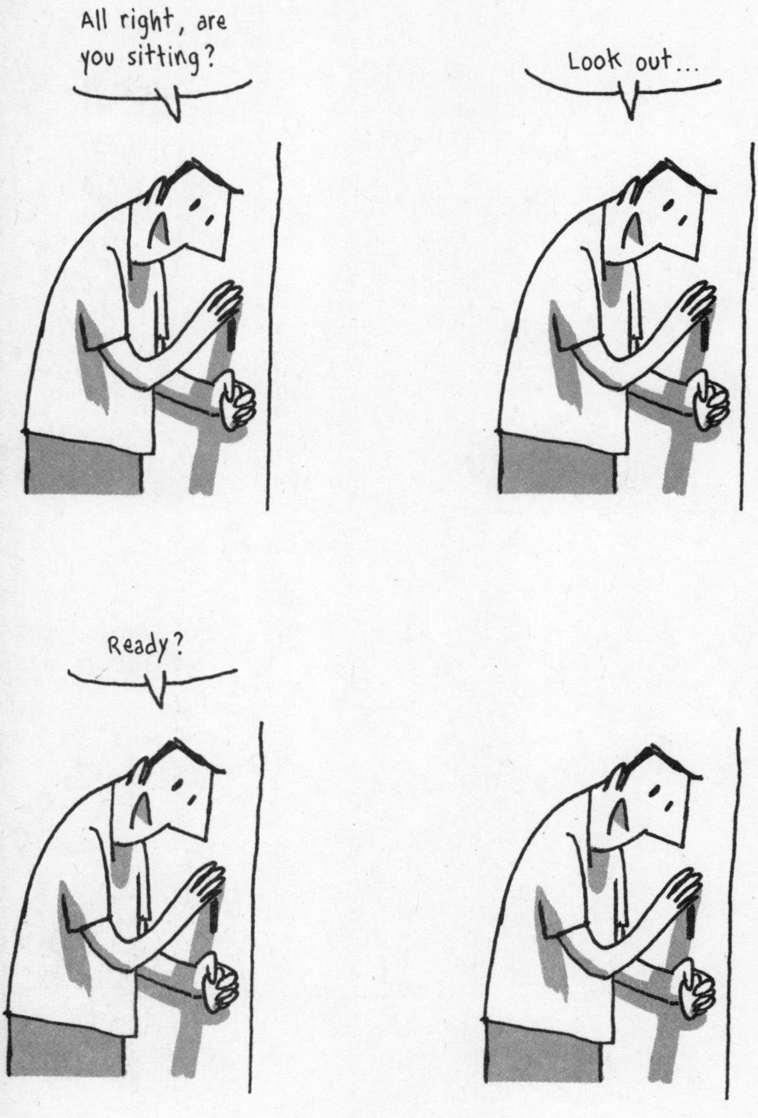
All right, are you sitting?
Look out...
Ready?

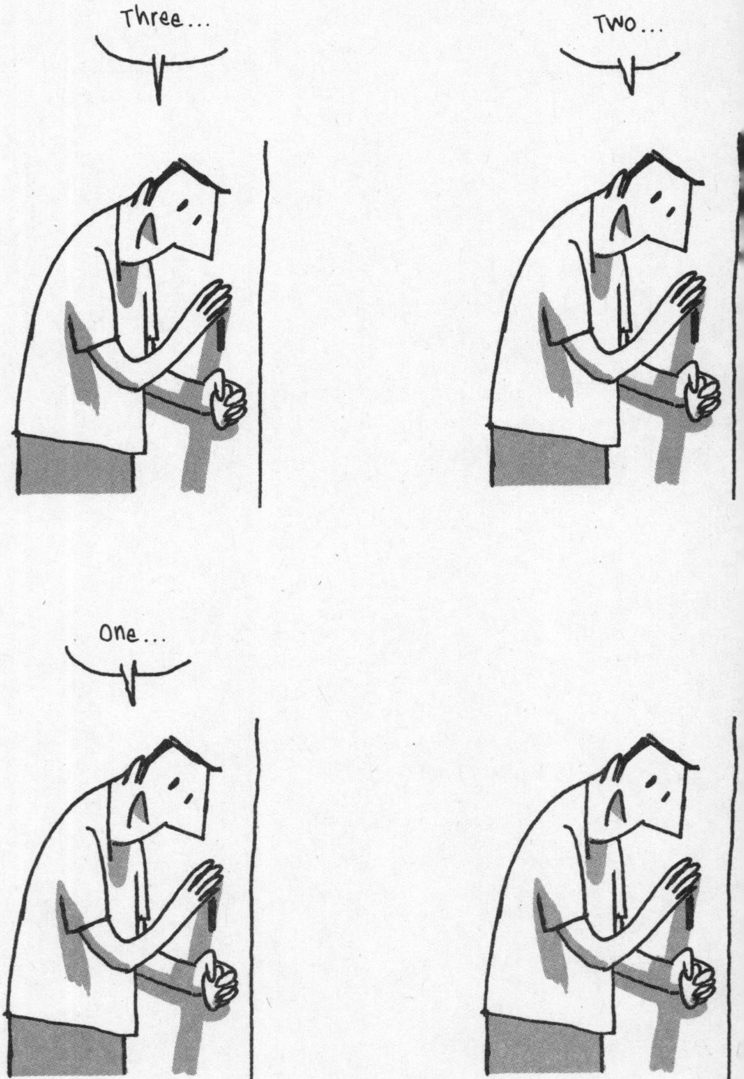
Three...
Two...
One...

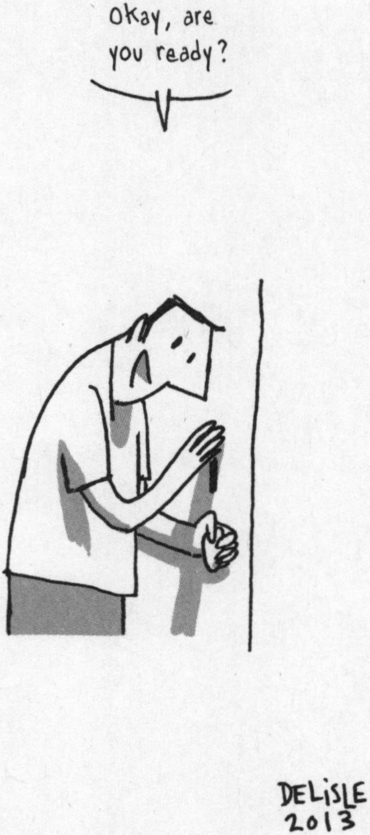
Okay, are you ready?
DELISLE 2013

-A Night at the B&B

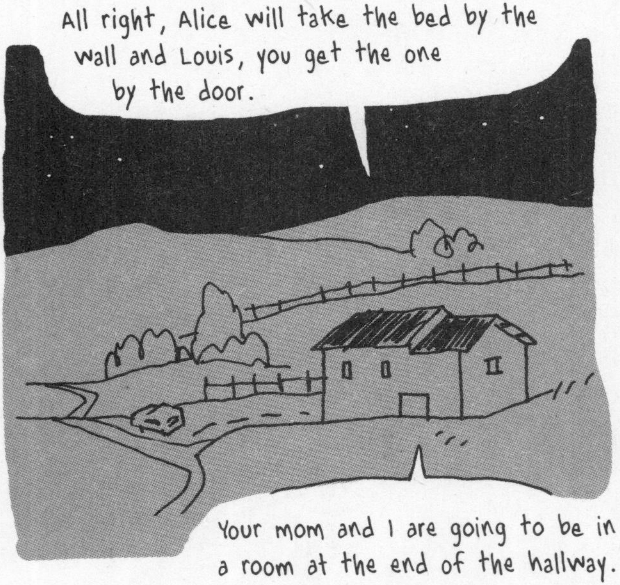
All right, Alice will take the bed by the wall and Louis, you get the one by the door.
Your mom and I are going to be in a room at the end of the hallway.

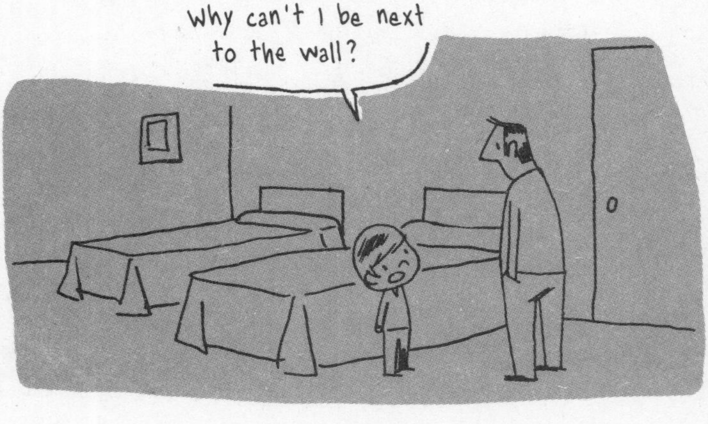
Why can't I be next to the wall?

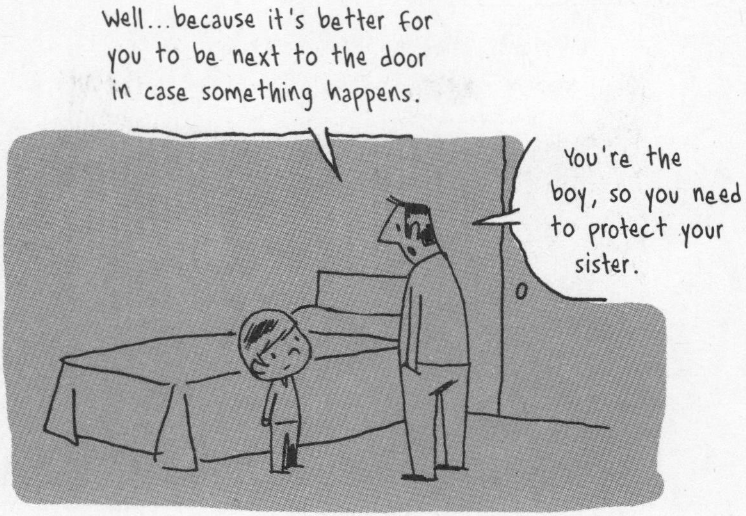
Well...because it's better for you to be next to the door in case something happens.
You're the boy, so you need to protect your sister.

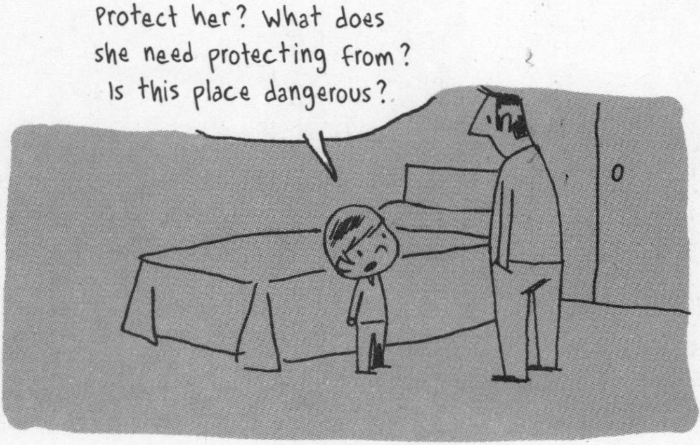
Protect her? What does she need protecting from? Is this place dangerous?

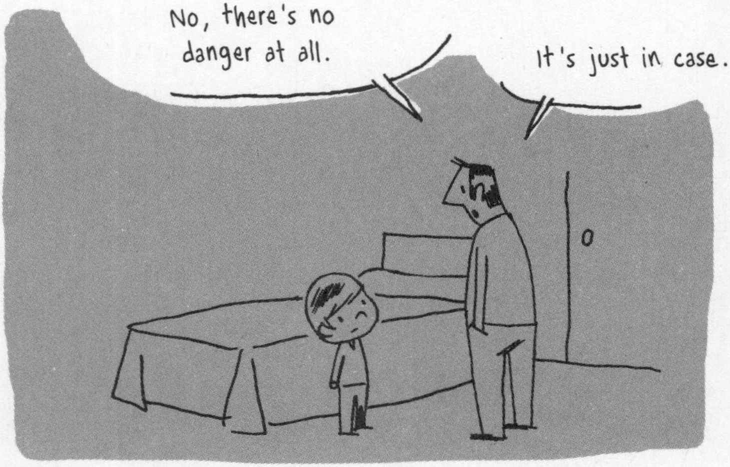
No, there's no danger at all.
It's just in case.

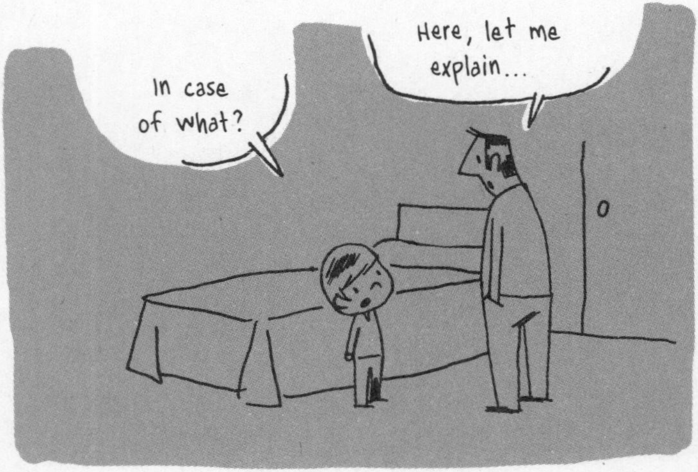
In case of what?
Here, let me explain...

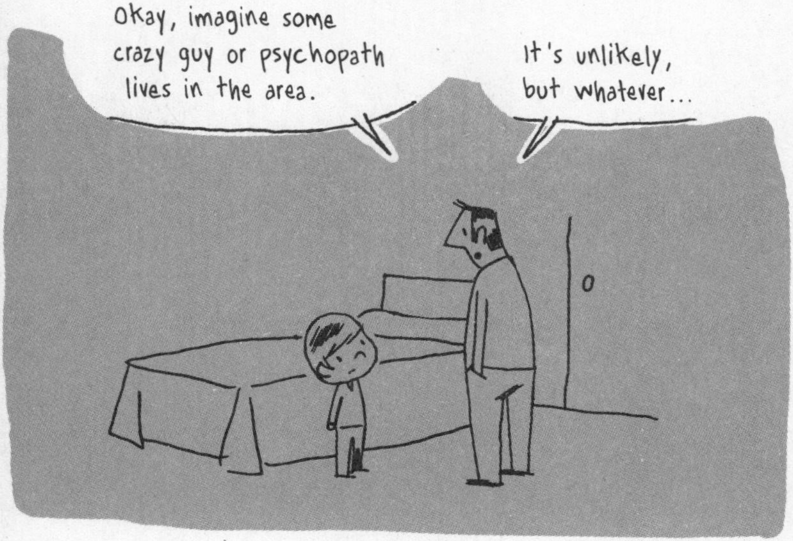
Okay, imagine some crazy guy or psychopath lives in the area.
It's unlikely, but whatever...

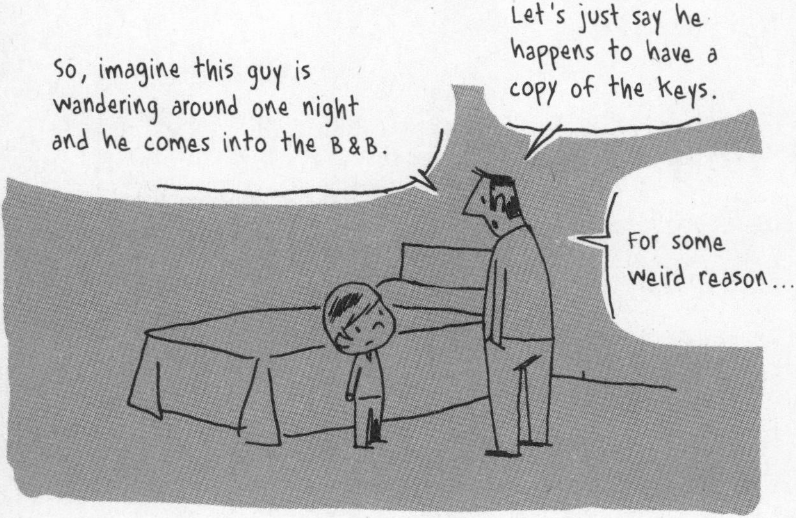
So, imagine this guy is wandering around one night and he comes into the B&B.
Let's just say he happens to have a copy of the keys.
For some weird reason...

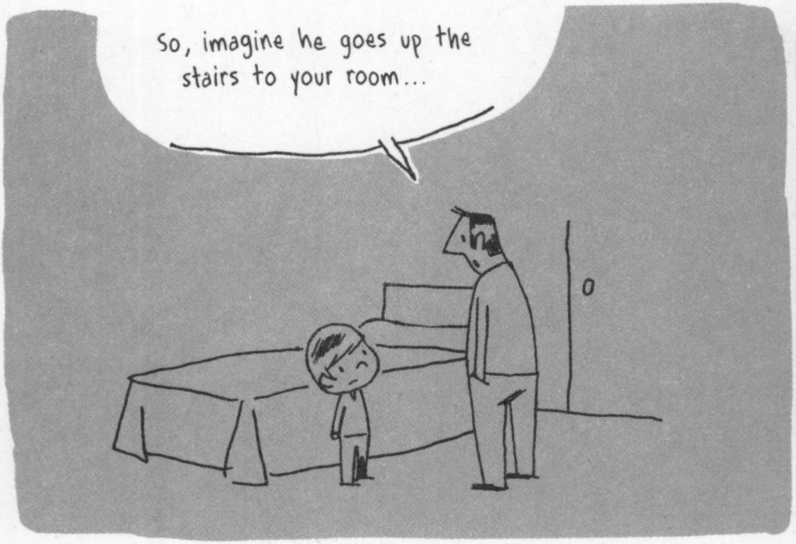
So, imagine he goes up the stairs to your room...

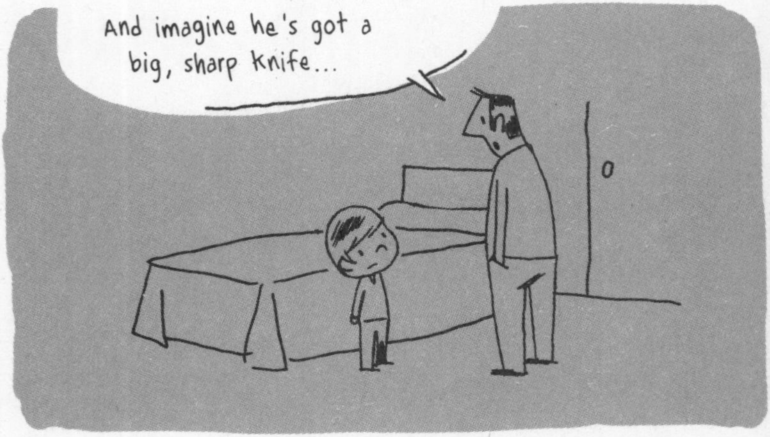
And imagine he's got a big, sharp knife...

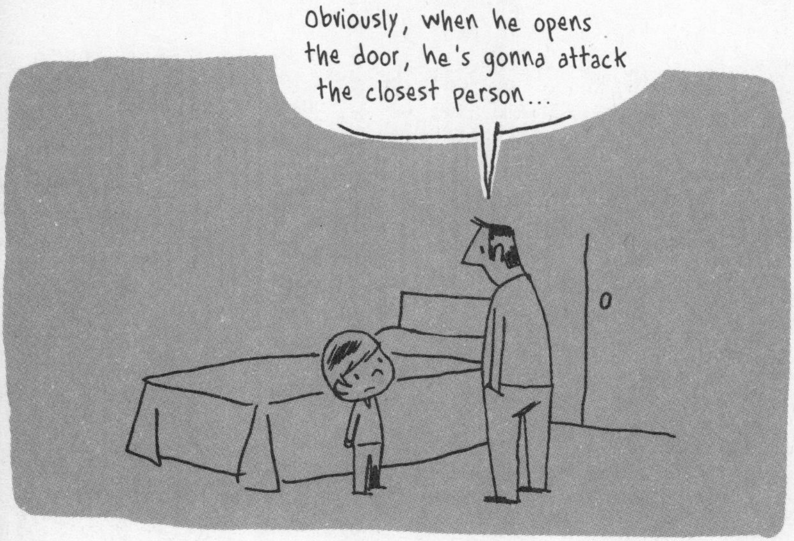
Obviously, when he opens the door, he's gonna attack the closest person...

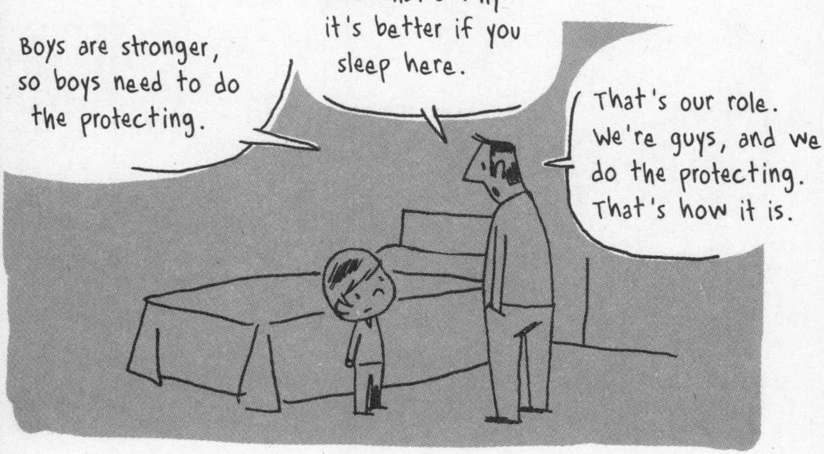
Boys are stronger, so boys need to do the protecting.
And that's why it's better if you sleep here.
That's our role. We're guys, and we do the protecting. That's how it is.

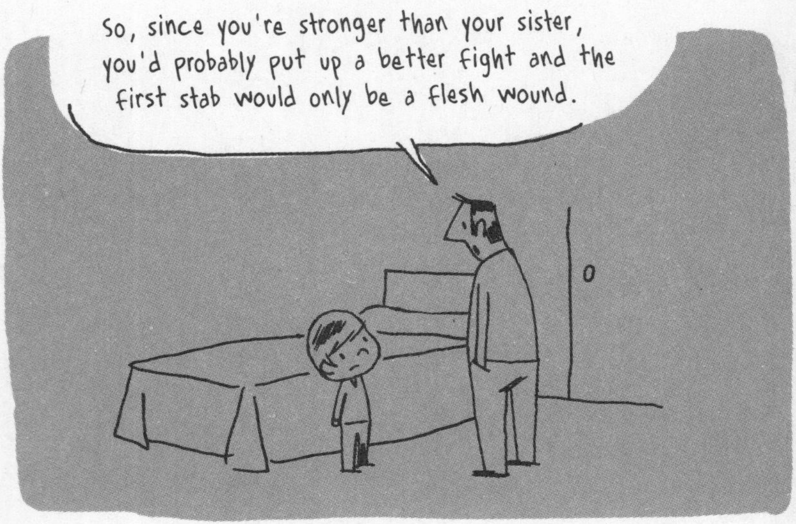
So, since you're stronger than your sister, you'd probably put up a better fight and the first stab would only be a flesh wound.

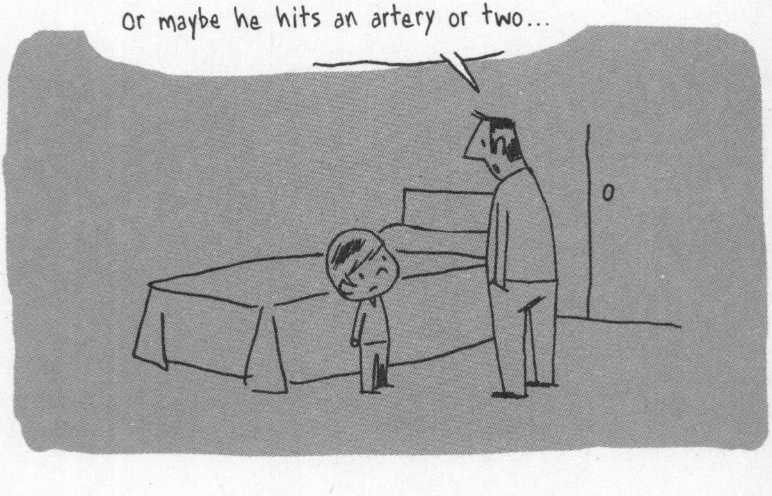
Or maybe he hits an artery or two...

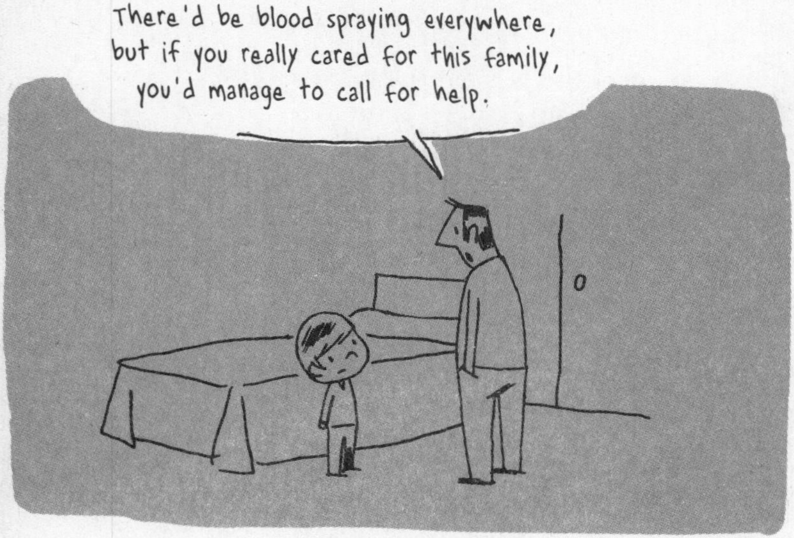
There'd be blood spraying everywhere, but if you really cared for this family, you'd manage to call for help.

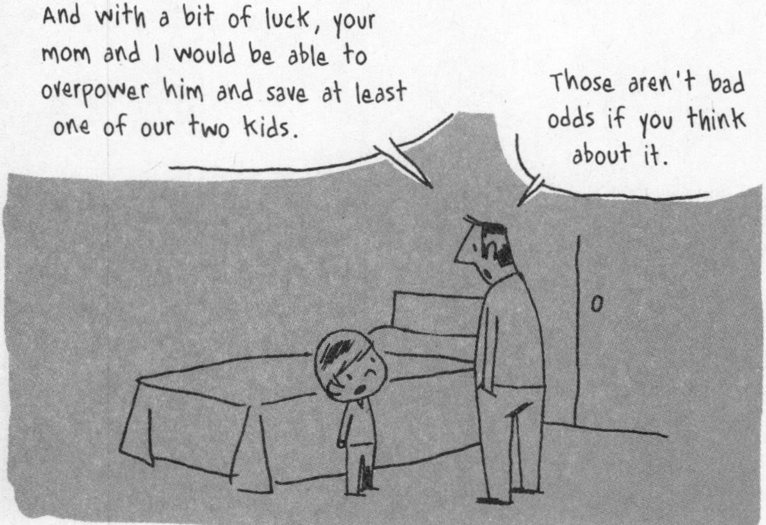
And with a bit of luck, your mom and I would be able to overpower him and save at least one of our two kids.
Those aren't bad odds if you think about it.

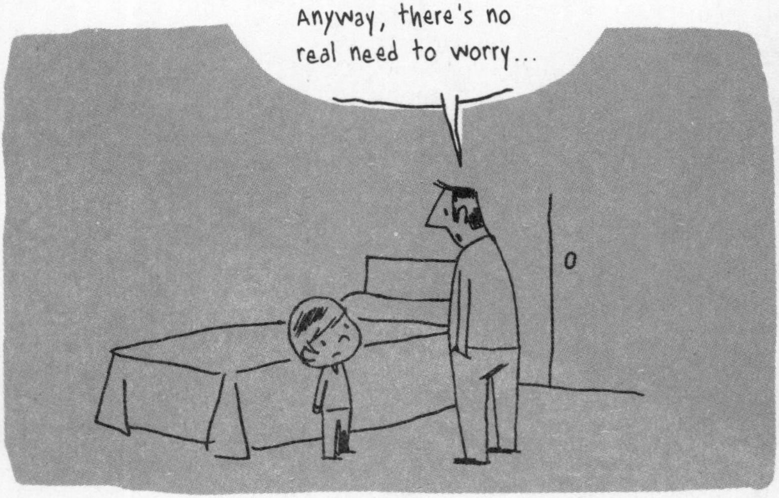
Anyway, there's no real need to worry...

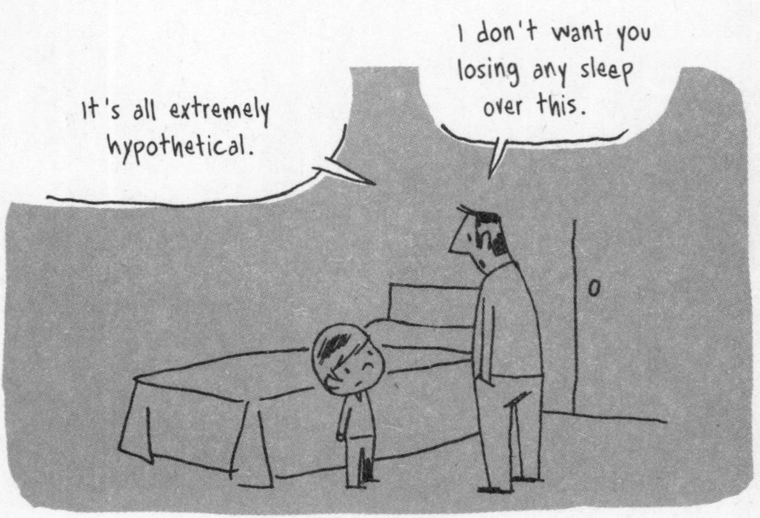
It's all extremely hypothetical.
I don't want you losing any sleep over this.

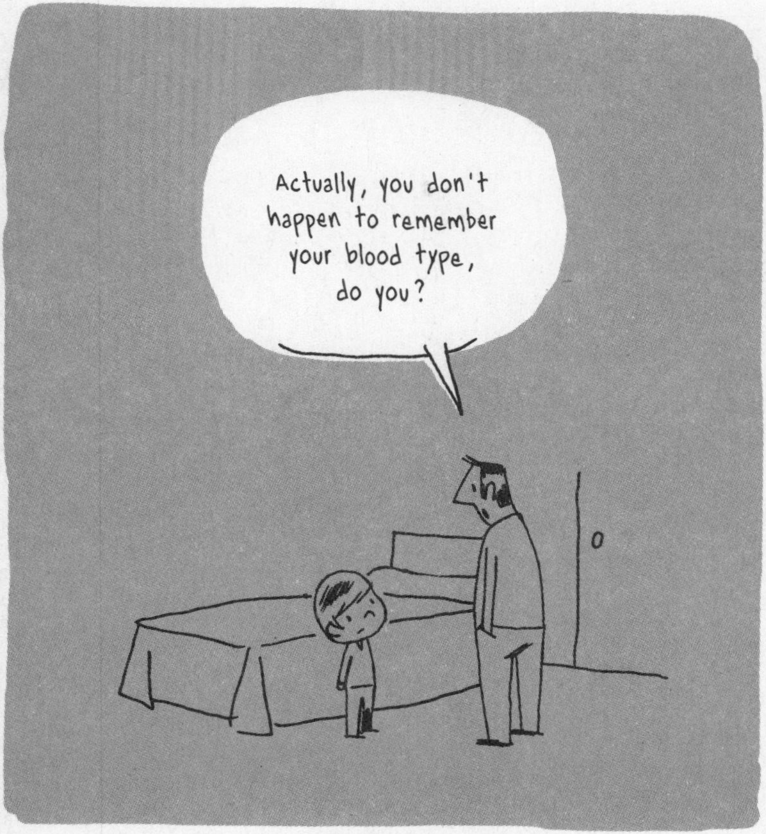
Actually, you don't happen to remember your blood type, do you?

DELISLE
2013

-The Piñata

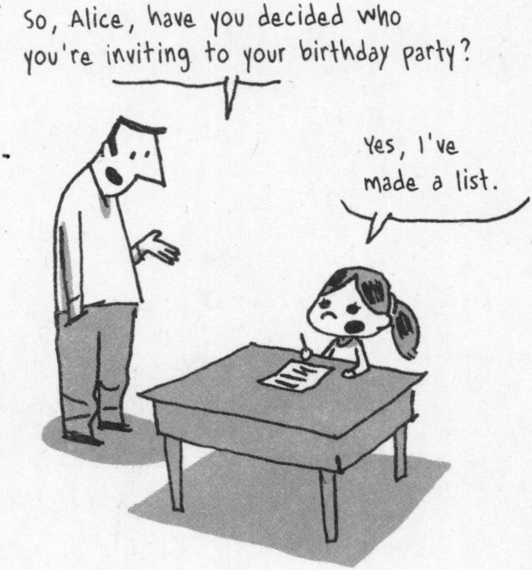
So, Alice, have you decided who you're inviting to your birthday party?
Yes, I've made a list.

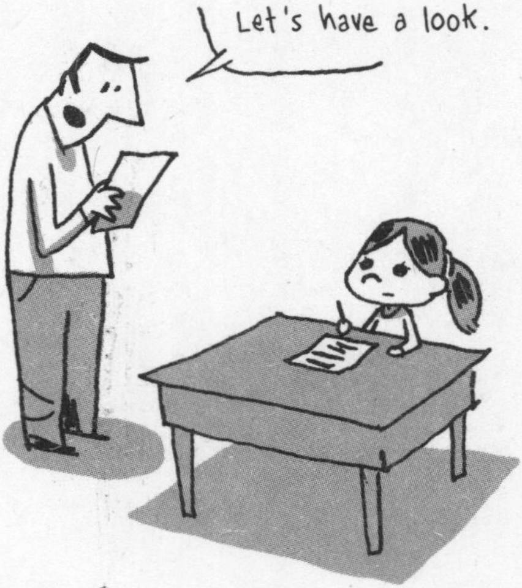
Let's have a look.

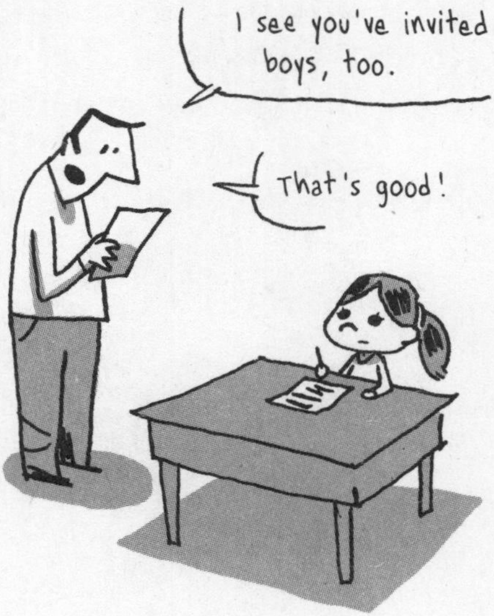
I see you've invited boys, too.
That's good!

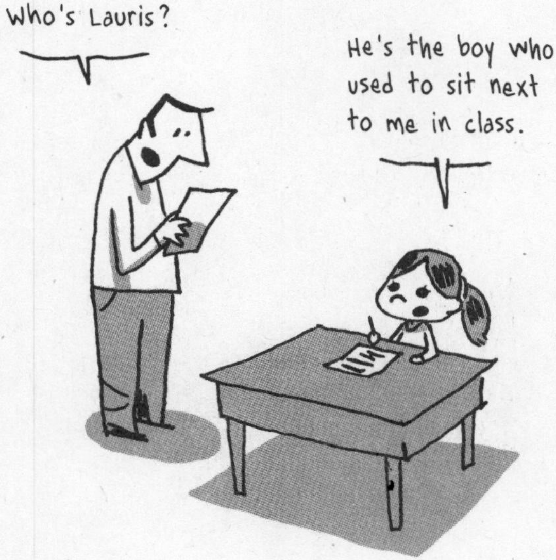
Who's Lauris?
He's the boy who used to sit next to me in class.

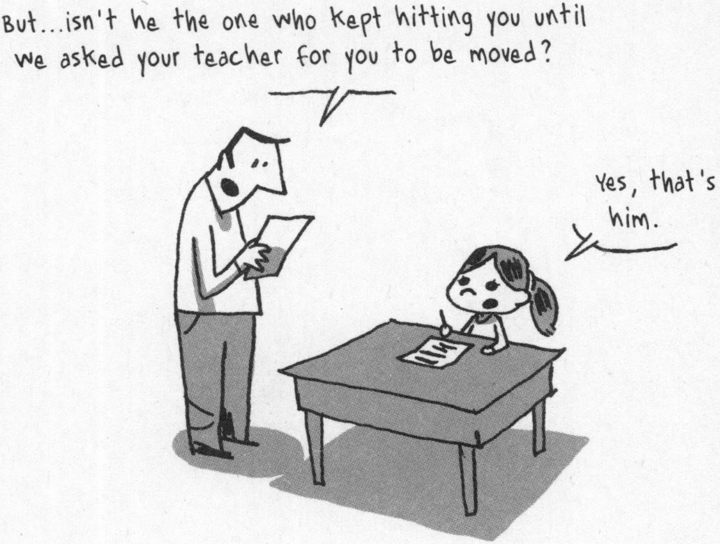
But...isn't he the one who kept hitting you until we asked your teacher for you to be moved?
Yes, that's him.

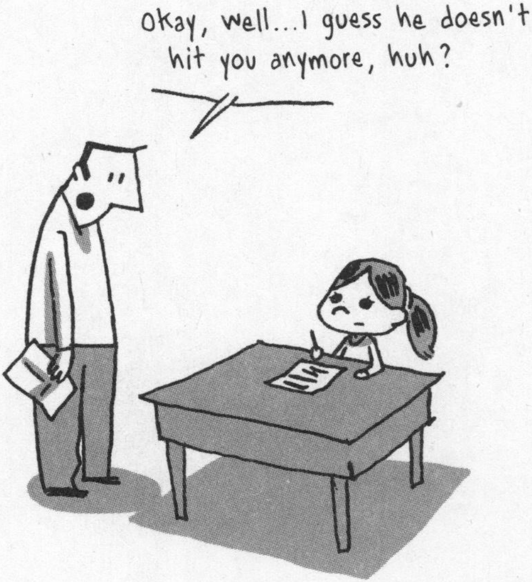
Okay, well...I guess he doesn't hit you anymore, huh?

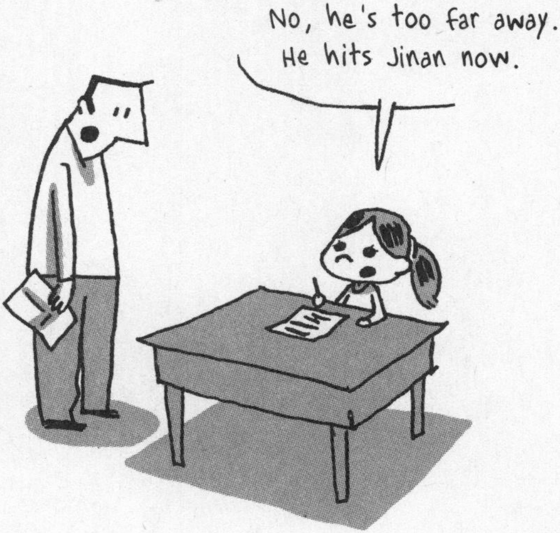
No, he's too far away. He hits Jinan now.

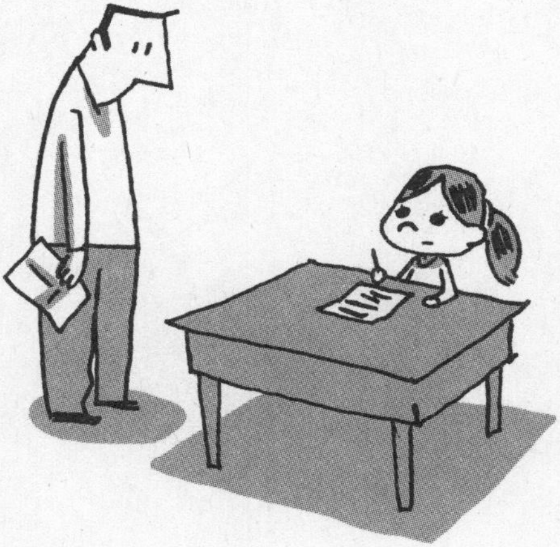

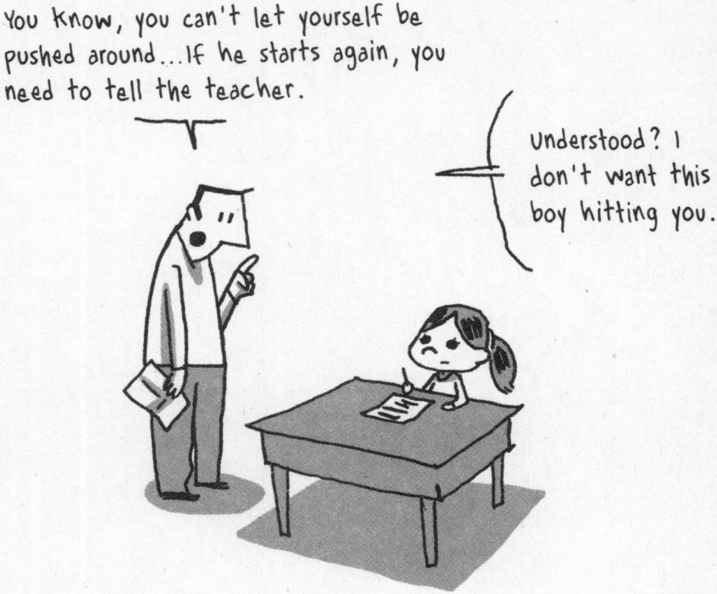
You know, you can't let yourself be pushed around... If he starts again, you need to tell the teacher.
Understood? I don't want this boy hitting you.

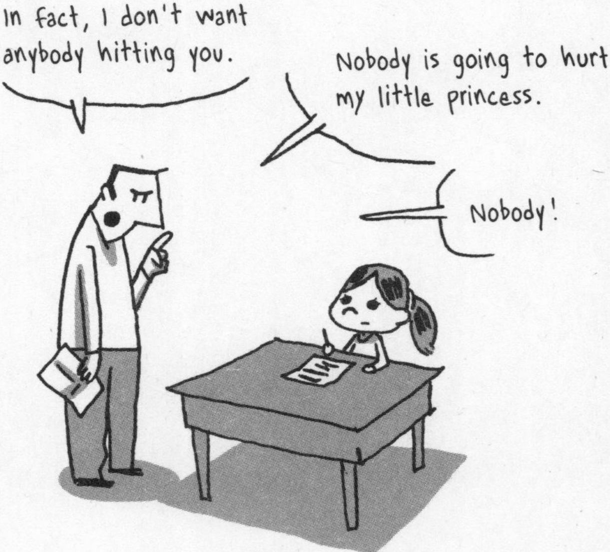
In fact, I don't want anybody hitting you.
Nobody is going to hurt my little princess.
Nobody!

Alice's birthday

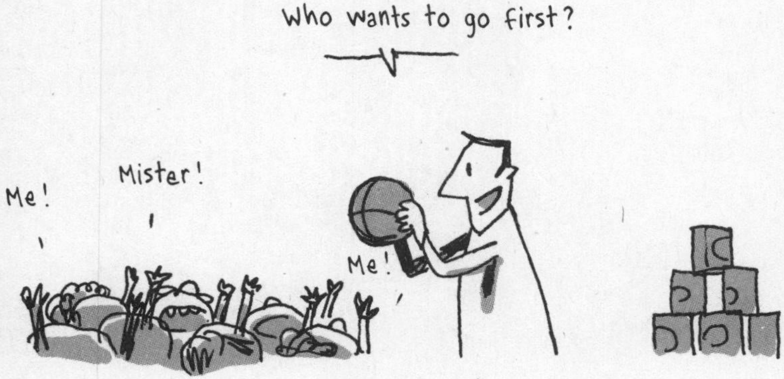
Who wants to go first?
Me!
Mister!
Me!

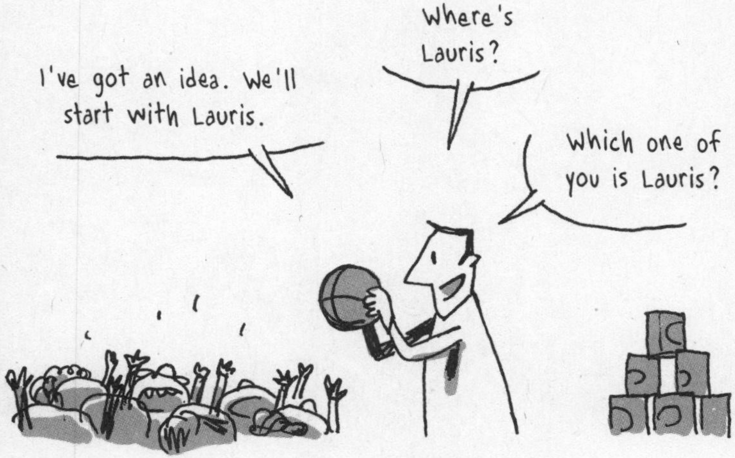
I've got an idea. We'll start with Lauris.
Where's Lauris?
Which one of you is Lauris?

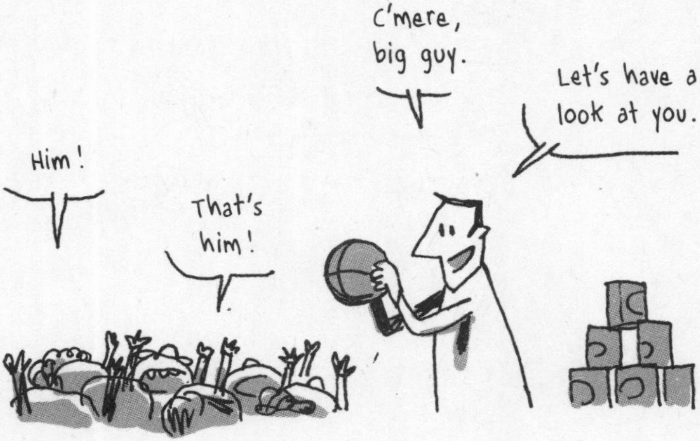
Him!
That's him!
C'mere, big guy.
Let's have a look at you.

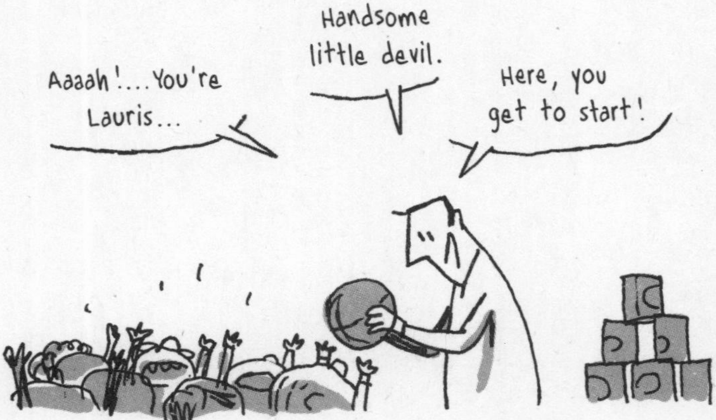
Handsome little devil.
Here, you get to start!
Aaaah!.... You're Lauris...

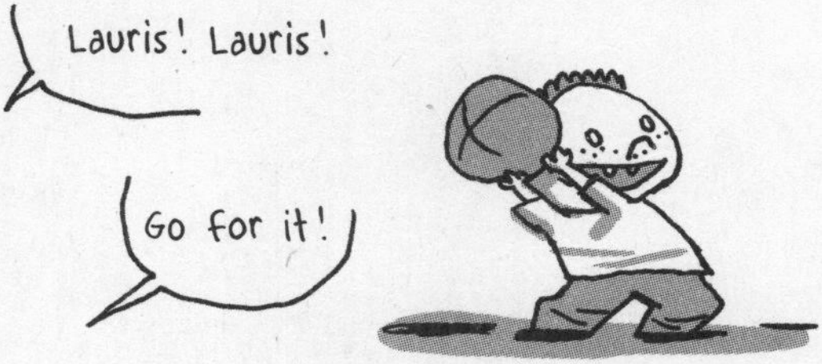
Lauris! Lauris!
Go for it!

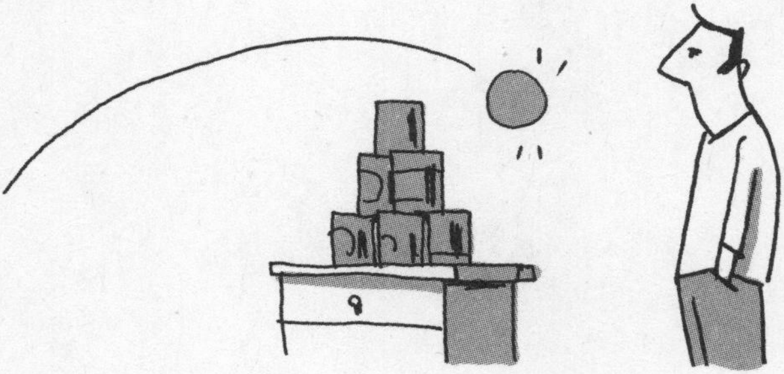

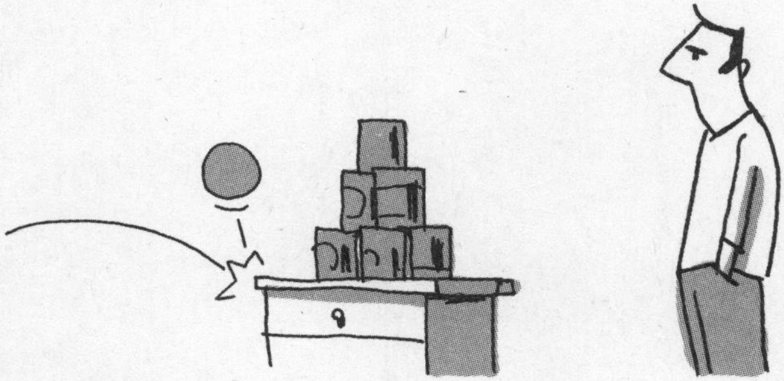

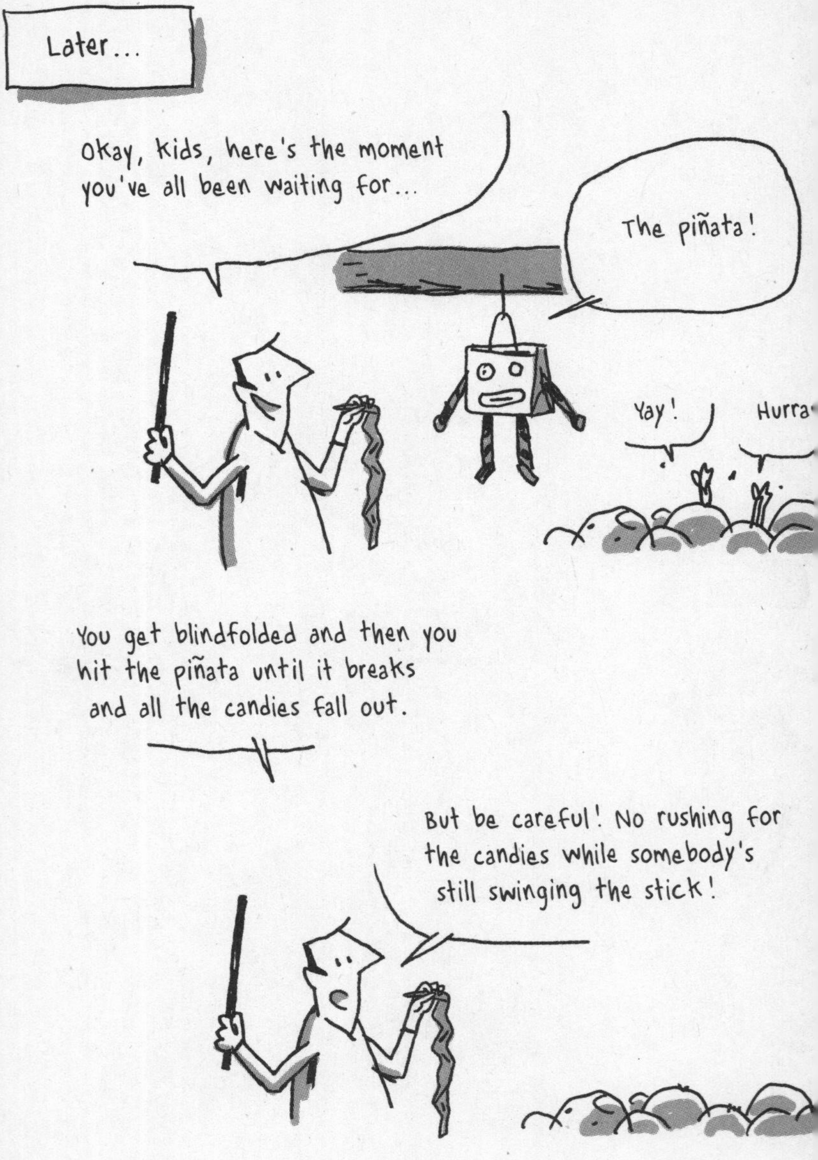
Later...
Okay, kids, here's the moment you've all been waiting for...
The piñata!
Yay!
Hurra
You get blindfolded and then you hit the piñata until it breaks and all the candies fall out.
But be careful! No rushing for the candies while somebody's still swinging the stick!

It's dangerous!
Very dangerous!

Alice
Yaniic
Lison

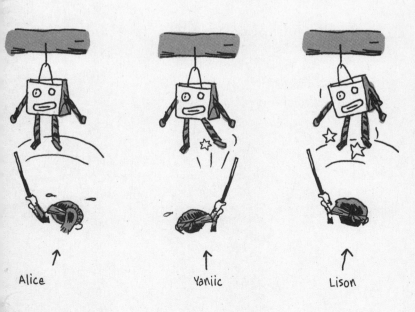

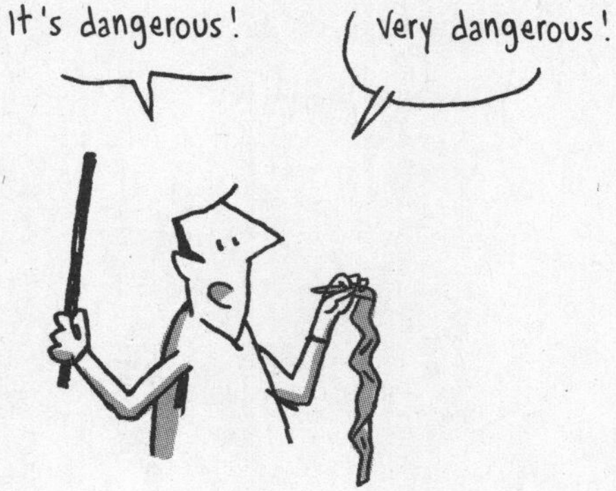

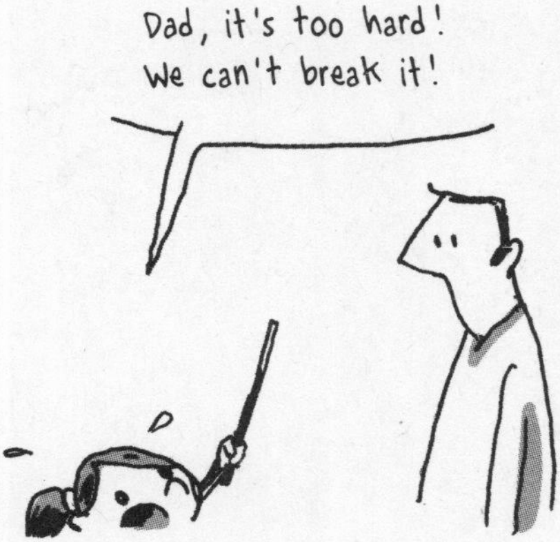
Dad, it's too hard! We can't break it!

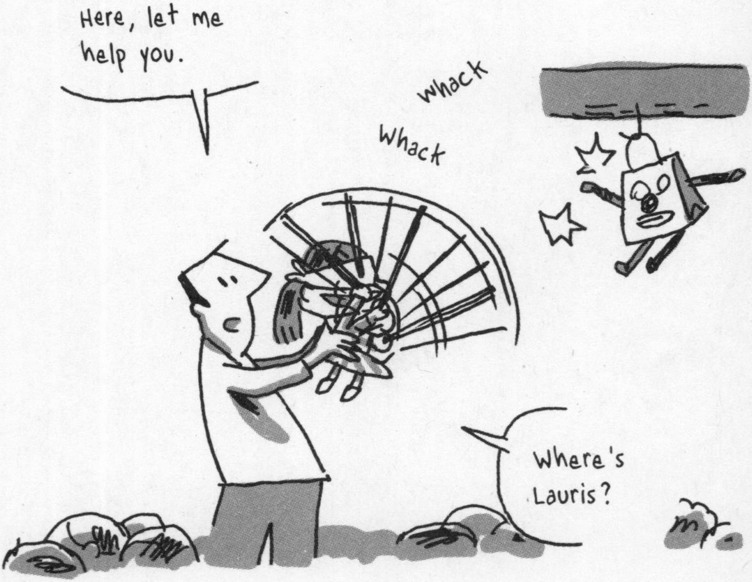
Here, let me help you.
whack
Whack
Where's Lauris?

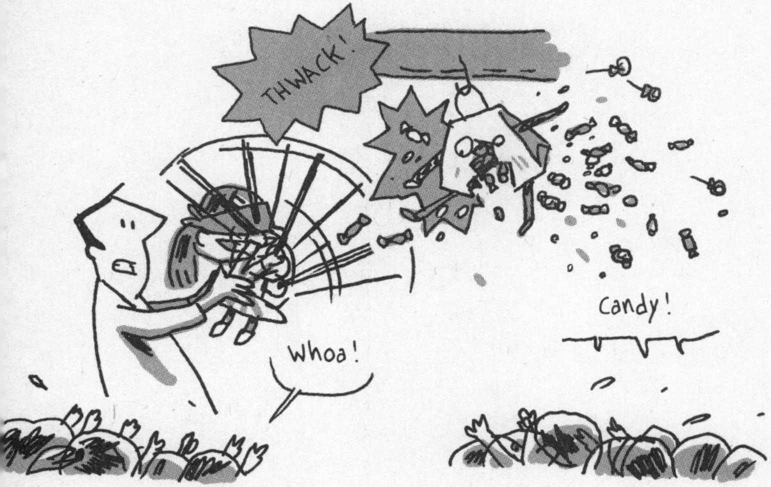
THWACK!
Whoa!
Candy!

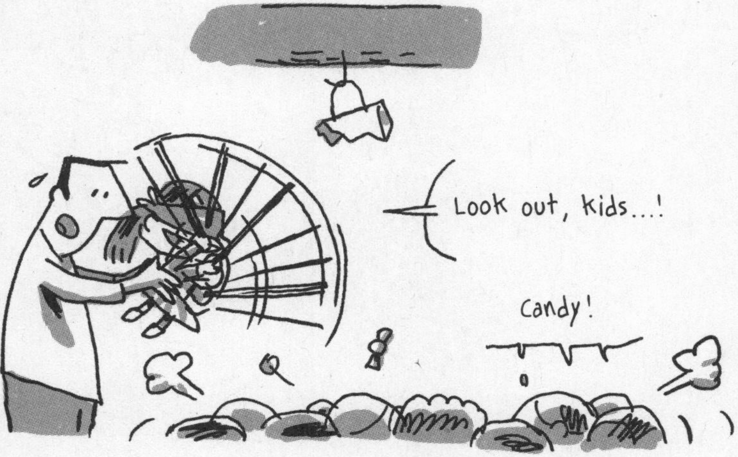
Look out, kids...!
Candy!

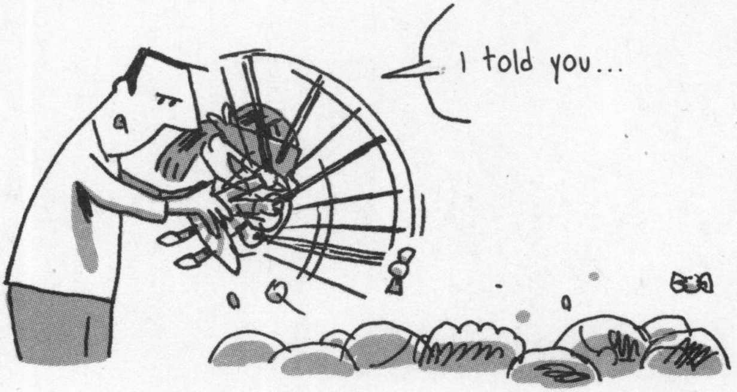
I told you...

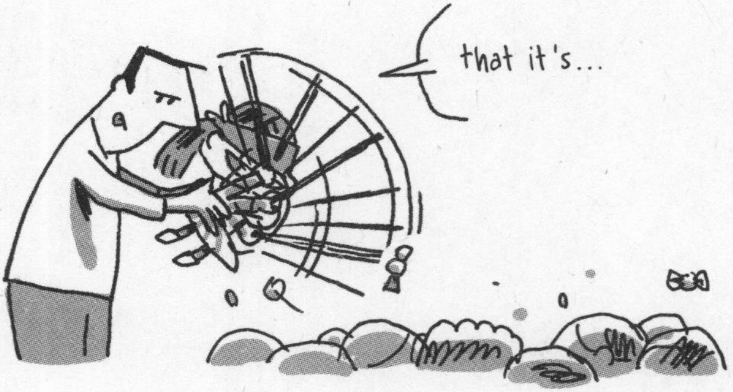
that it's...

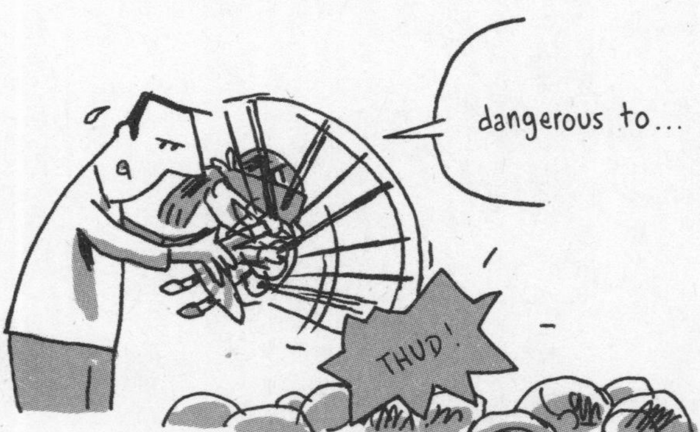
dangerous to...
THUD!

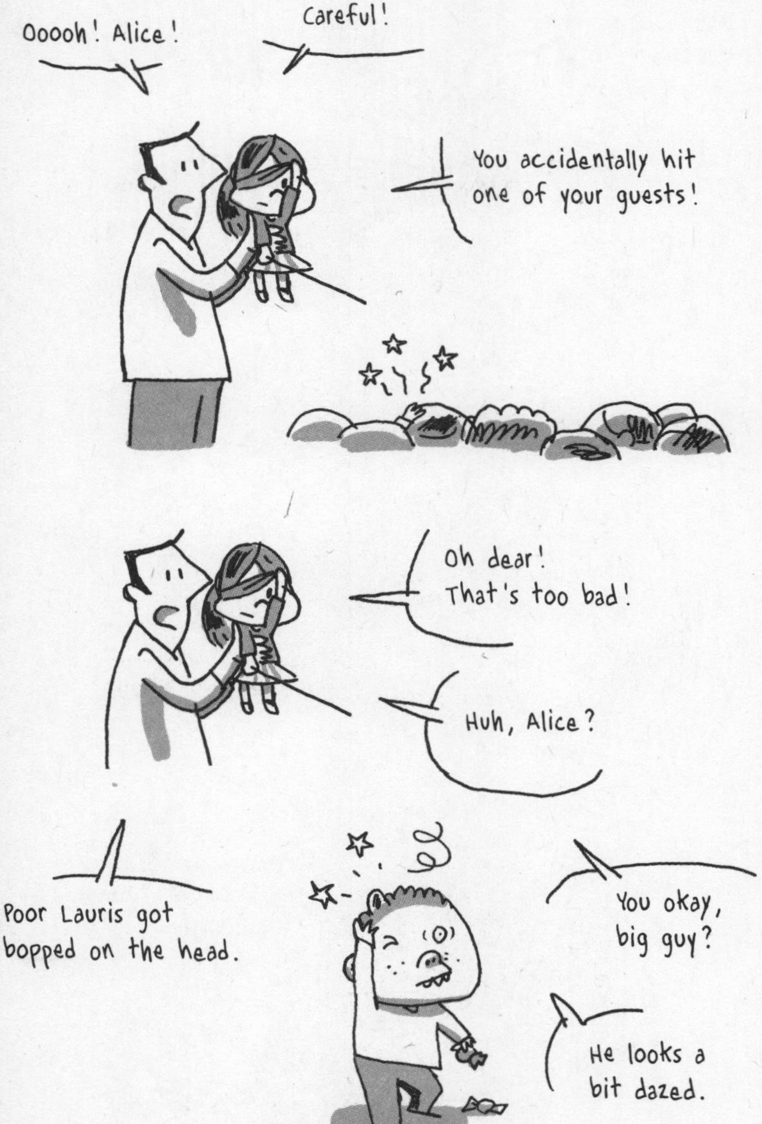
Ooooh! Alice!
Careful!
You accidentally hit one of your guests!
Oh dear! That's too bad!
Huh, Alice?
Poor Lauris got bopped on the head.
You okay, big guy?
He looks a bit dazed.

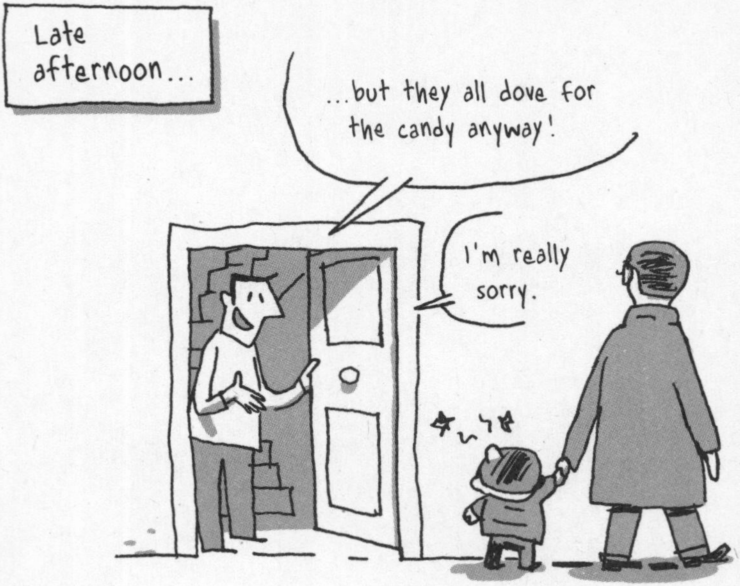
Late afternoon...
...but they all dove for the candy anyway!
I'm really sorry.

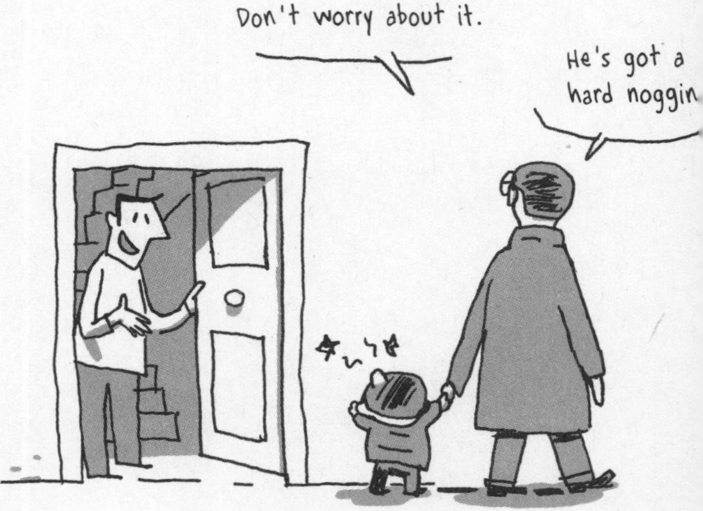
Don't worry about it.
He's got a hard noggin

DELISLE
2013

-Hide and Seek

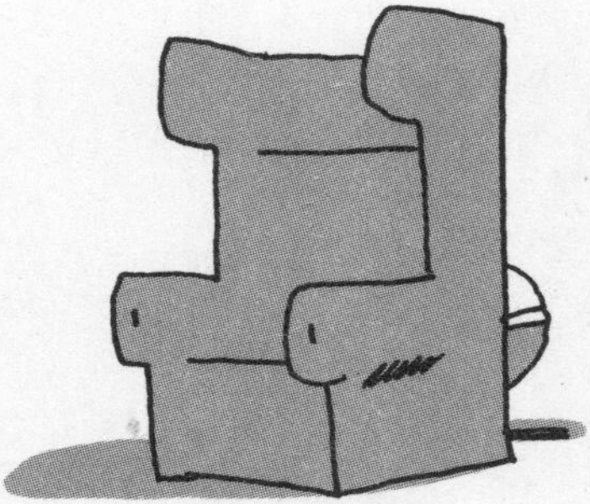

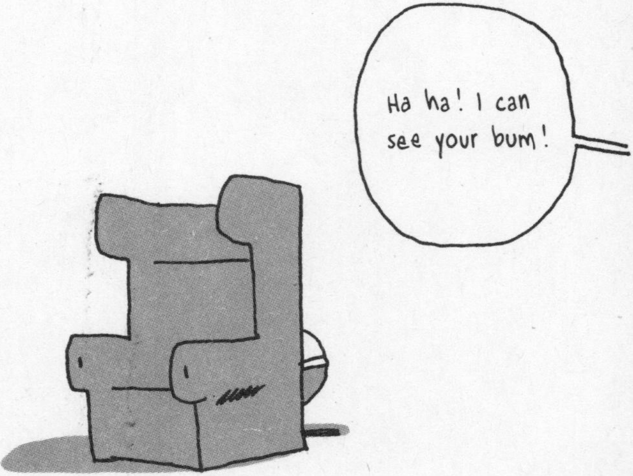
Ha ha! I can see your bum!

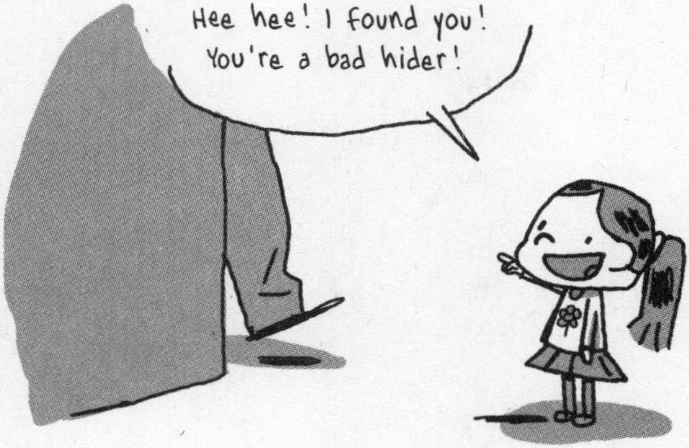
Hee hee! I found you! You're a bad hider!

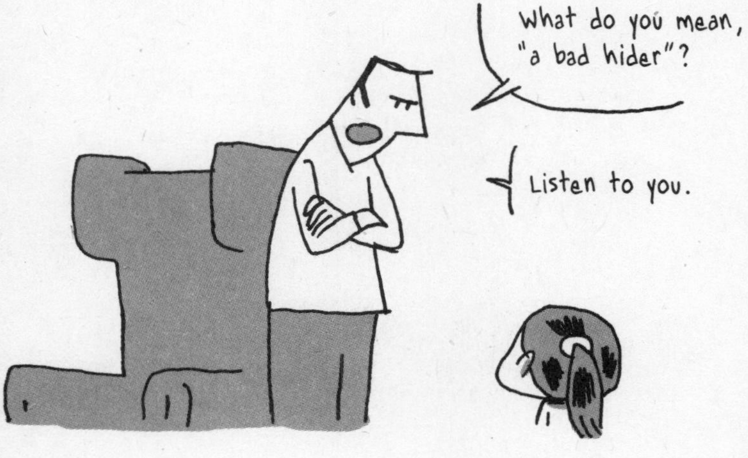
What do you mean, "a bad hider"?
Listen to you.

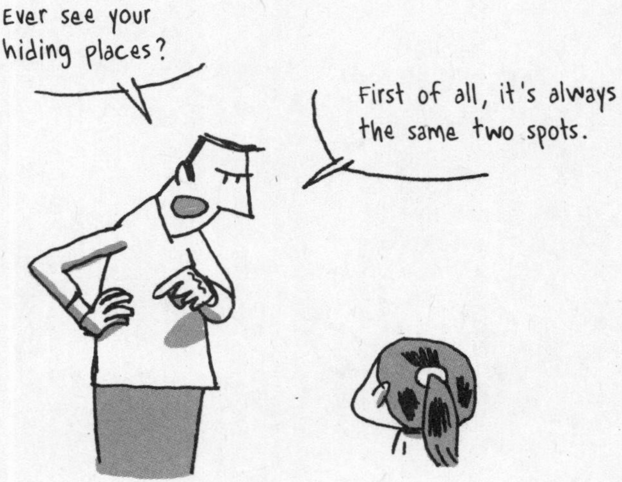
Ever see your hiding places?
First of all, it's always the same two spots.

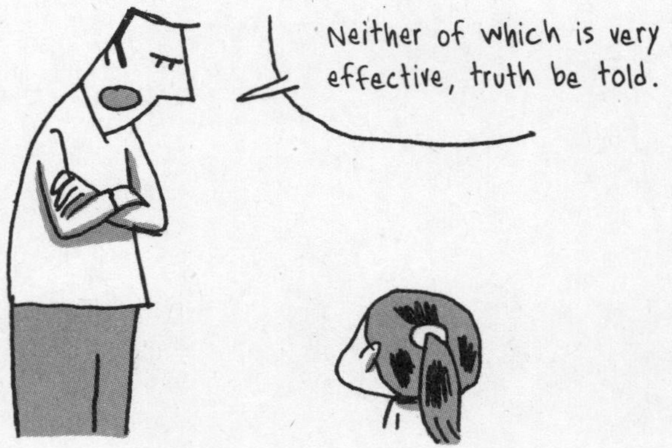
Neither of which is very effective, truth be told.

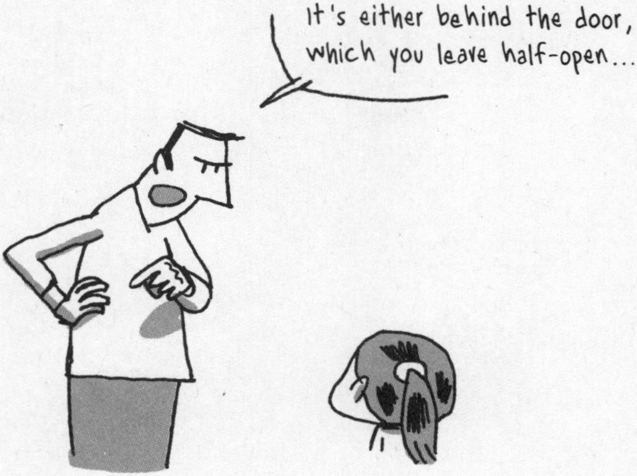
It's either behind the door, which you leave half-open...

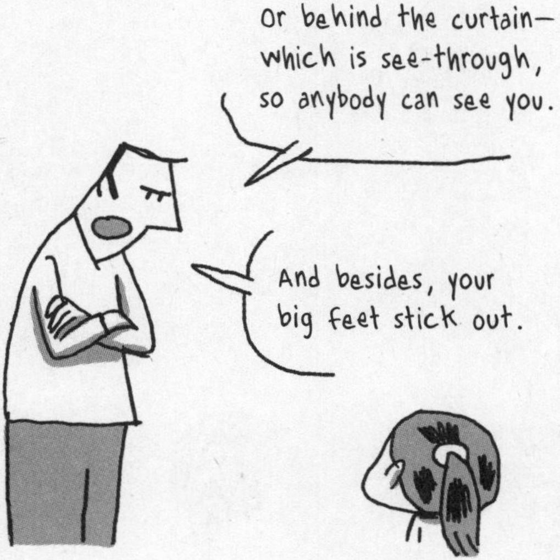
Or behind the curtain— which is see-through, so anybody can see you.
And besides, your big feet stick out.

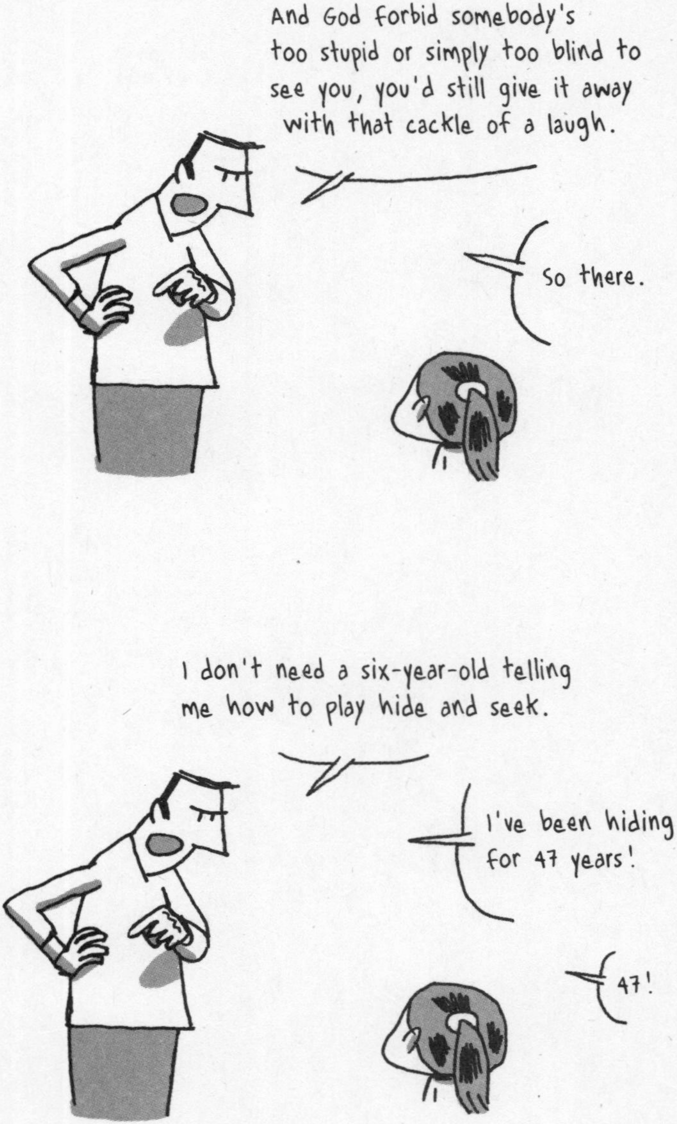
And God forbid somebody's too stupid or simply too blind to see you, you'd still give it away with that cackle of a laugh.
So there.
I don't need a six-year-old telling me how to play hide and seek.
I've been hiding for 47 years!
47!

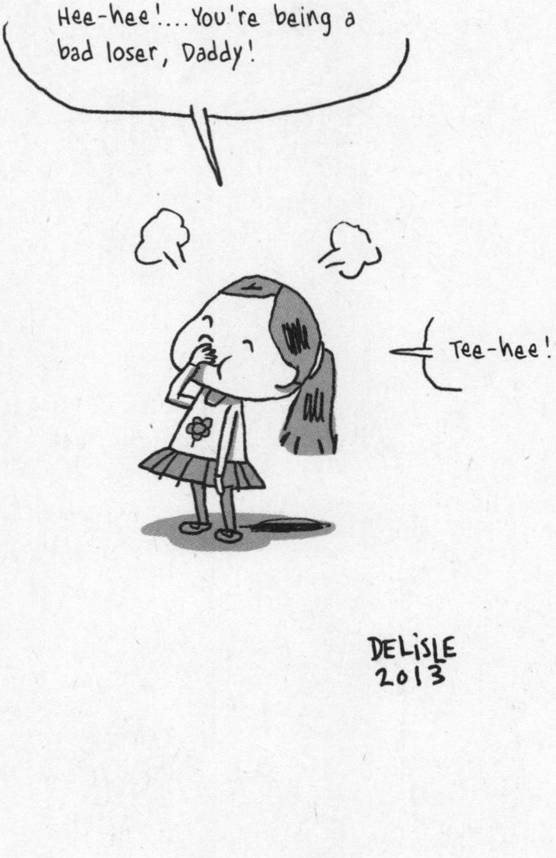
Hee-hee!... You're being a bad loser, Daddy!
Tee-hee!
DELISLE 2013

-Warcraft II

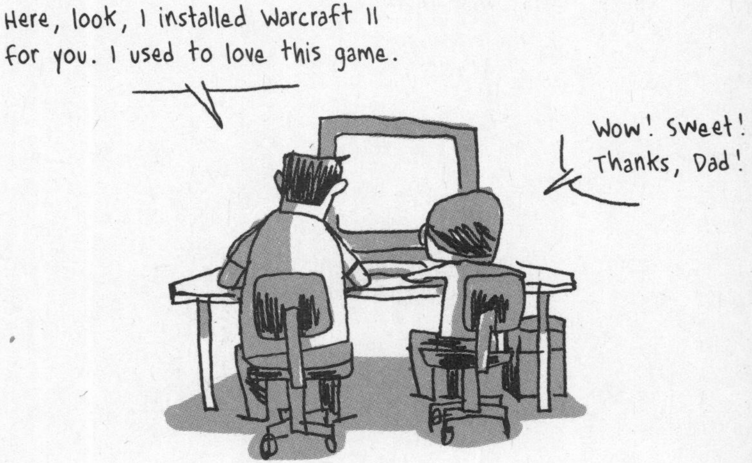
Here, look, I installed Warcraft II for you. I used to love this game.
Wow! Sweet! Thanks, Dad!

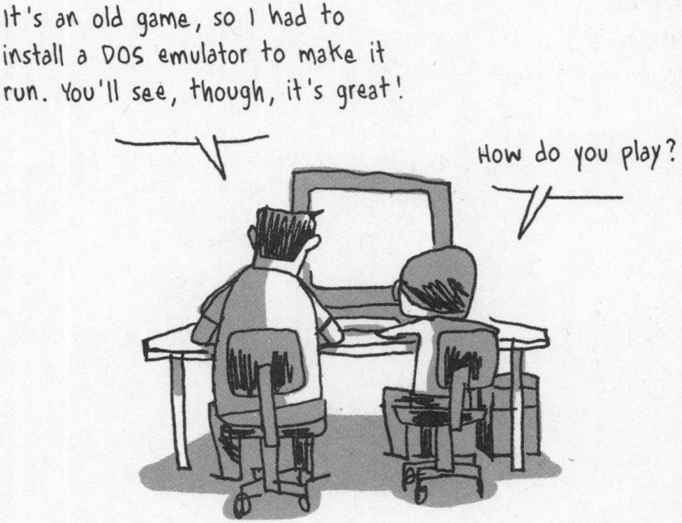
It's an old game, so I had to install a DOS emulator to make it run. You'll see, though, it's great!
How do you play?

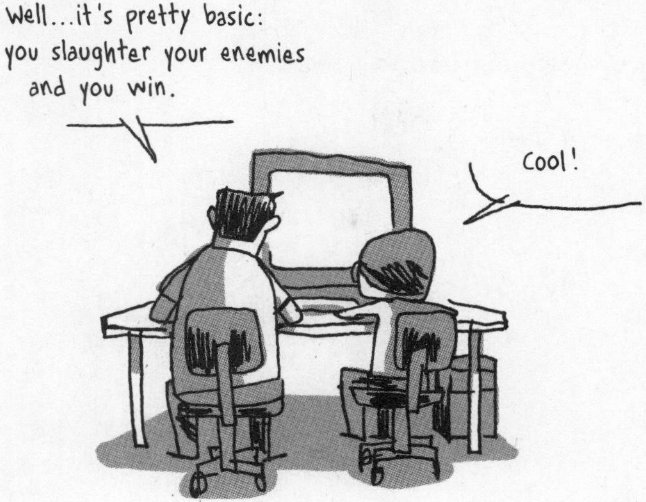
Well...it's pretty basic: you slaughter your enemies and you win.
Cool!
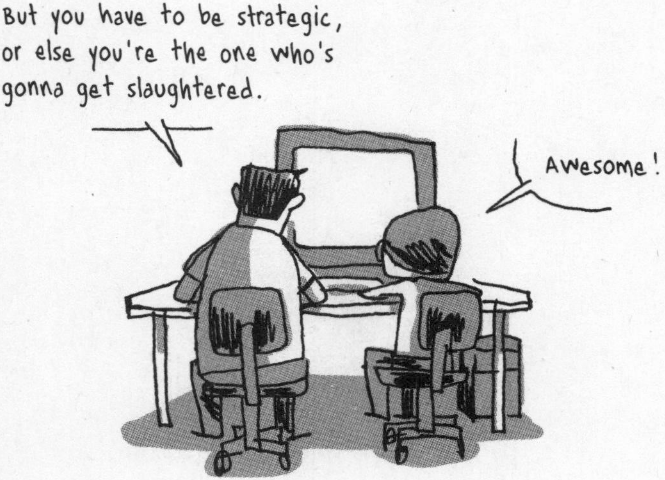
But you have to be strategic, or else you're the one who's gonna get slaughtered.
Awesome!

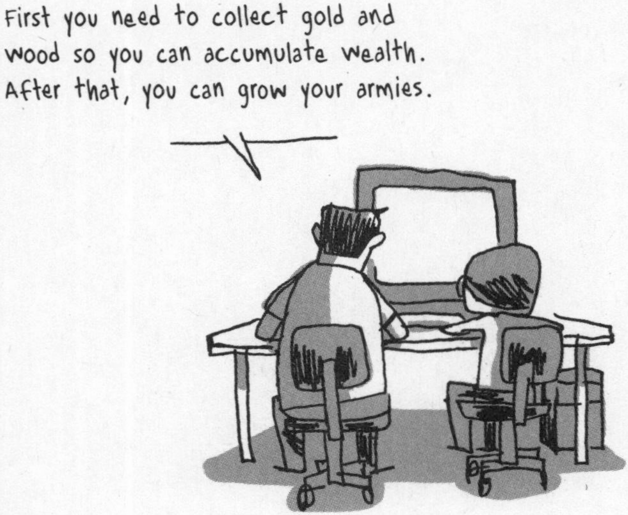
First you need to collect gold and wood so you can accumulate wealth. After that, you can grow your armies.

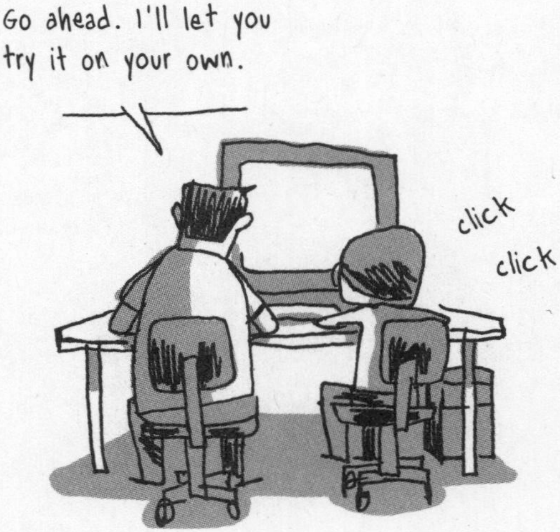
Go ahead. I'll let you try it on your own.
click
click

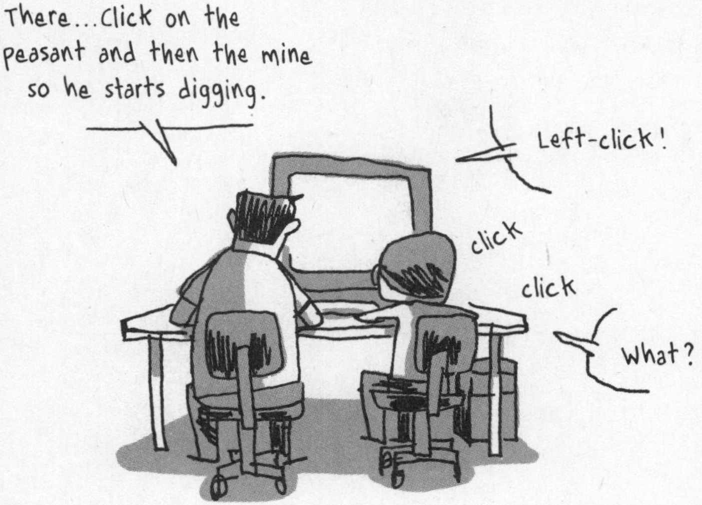
There...Click on the peasant and then the mine so he starts digging.
Left-click!
click
click
What?

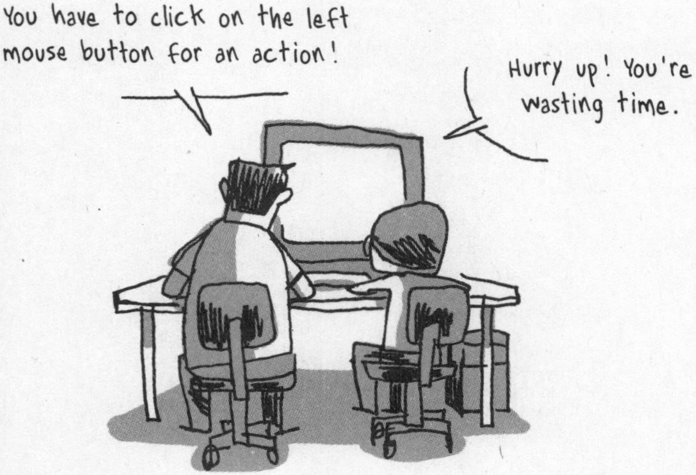
You have to click on the left mouse button for an action!
Hurry up! You're wasting time.

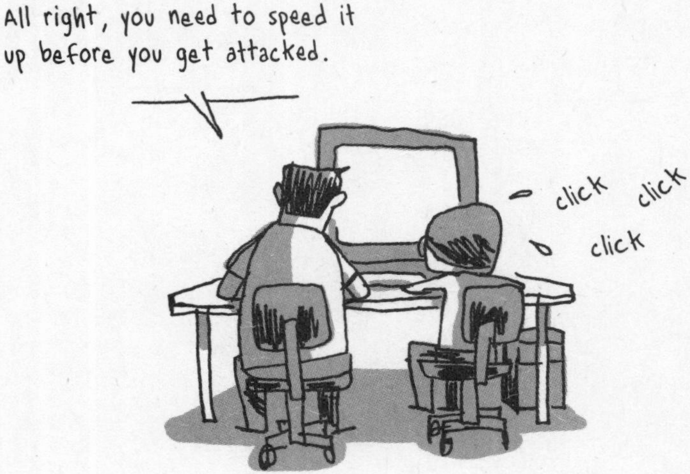
All right, you need to speed it up before you get attacked.
click click
click

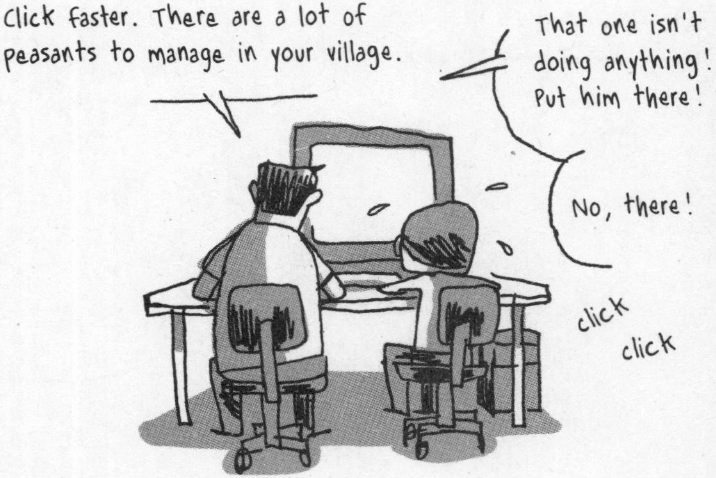
Click faster. There are a lot of peasants to manage in your village.
That one isn't doing anything! Put him there!
No, there!
click
click

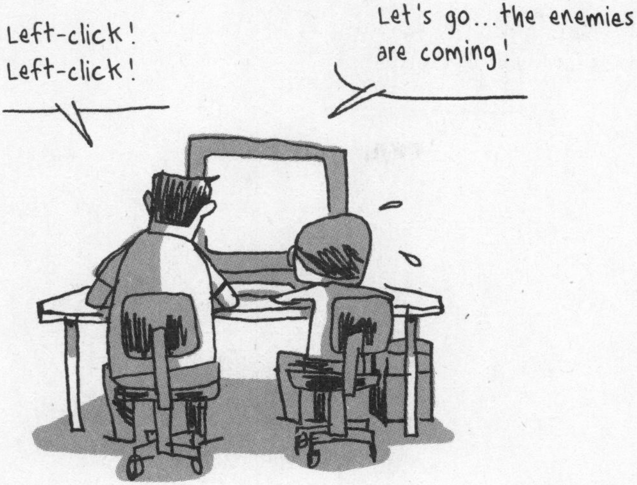
Left-click! Left-click!
Let's go...the enemies are coming!

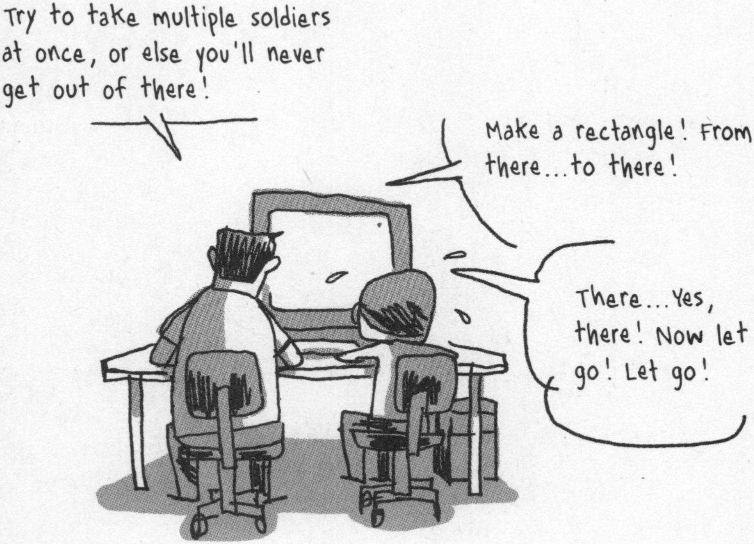
Try to take multiple soldiers at once, or else you'll never get out of there!
Make a rectangle! From there...to there!
There...Yes, there! Now let go! Let go!

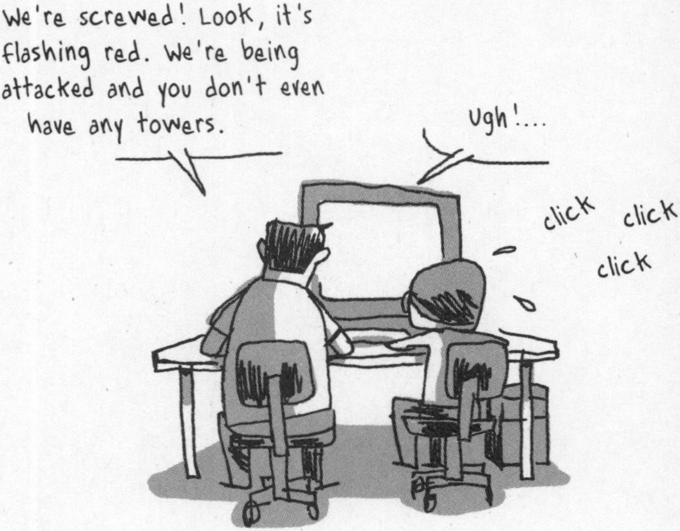
We're screwed! Look, it's flashing red. We're being attacked and you don't even have any towers.
Ugh!...
click
click
click

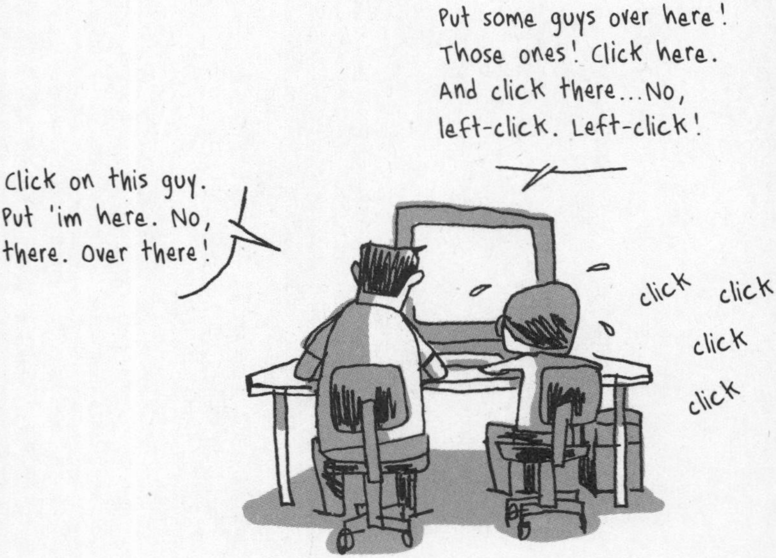
Put some guys over here! Those ones! Click here. And click there...No, left-click. Left-click!
Click on this guy. Put 'im here. No, there. Over there!
click
click
click
click

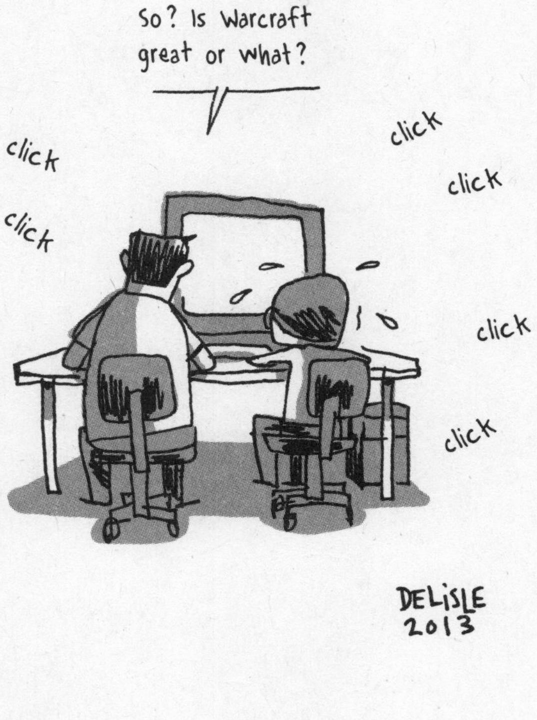
So? Is Warcraft great or what?
click
click
click
click
click
click
DELISLE 2013

-The Bookstore

Here, this is the manga section...They're often published in the original format, so you have to read them from right to left.

They've got all of Toriyama's books! Here's the series he created before Dragon Ball.

It's crazy stuff.

You should give it a try.

Oh! Look...Matsumoto.
Wow, that guy can draw!

The European books are over there.
They're often called "Franco-Belgian,"
but they're not just from France
and Belgium anymore.

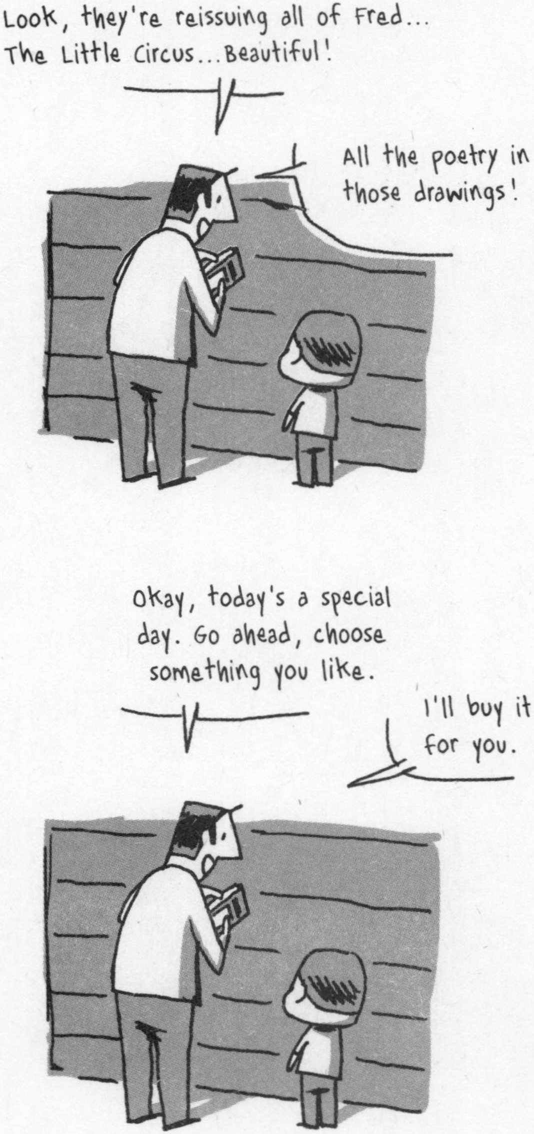
Look, they're reissuing all of Fred... The Little Circus...Beautiful!
All the poetry in those drawings!
Okay, today's a special day. Go ahead, choose something you like.
I'll buy it for you.

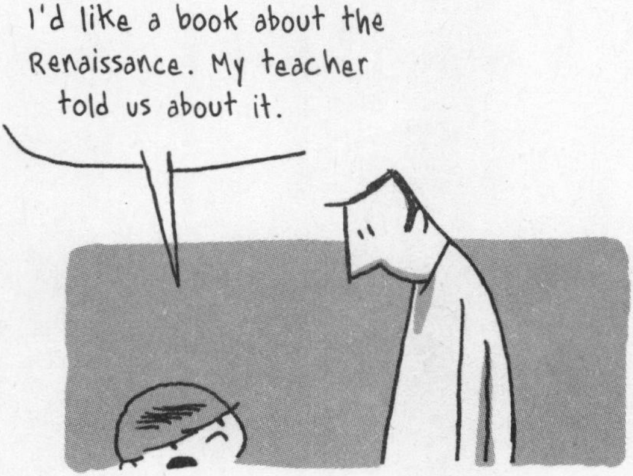
I'd like a book about the Renaissance. My teacher told us about it.

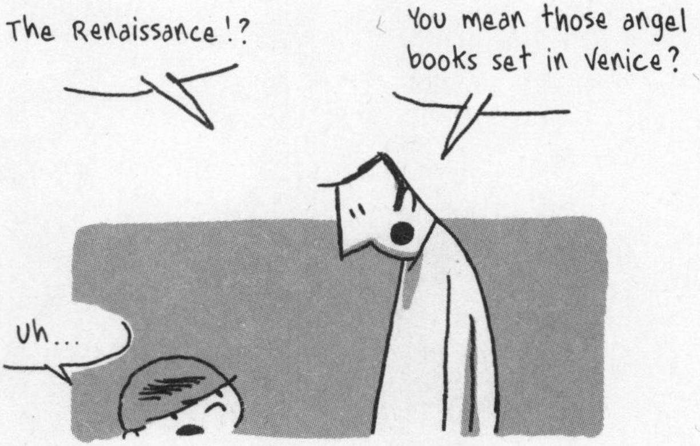
The Renaissance!?
You mean those angel books set in Venice?
Uh...

Hold on...are you talking
about a <u>real</u> book or
a comic?

I was thinking
about a book.

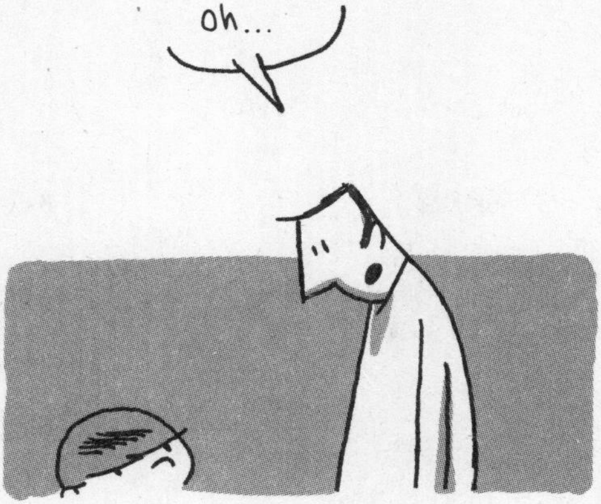
Oh...

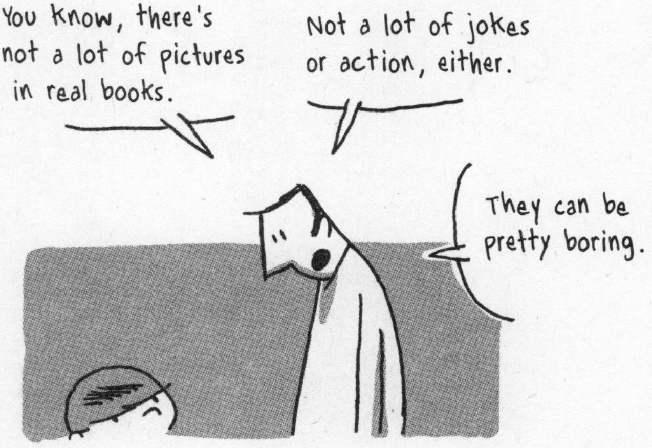
You know, there's not a lot of pictures in real books.
Not a lot of jokes or action, either.
They can be pretty boring.

Look, this is a specialized
bookstore. It only has comics.

And the closest normal
bookstore is on the other
side of town. So...

How about we try to find a
comic about the Renaissance?...

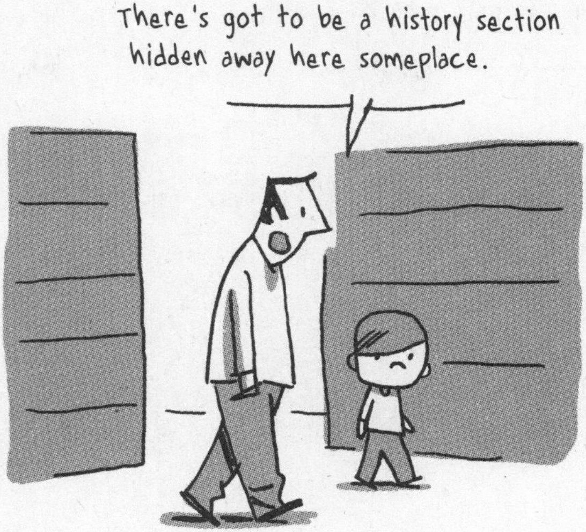
There's got to be a history section hidden away here someplace.

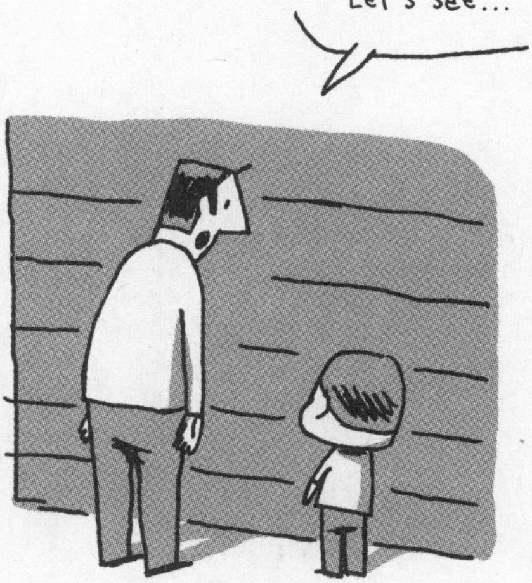
Let's see...

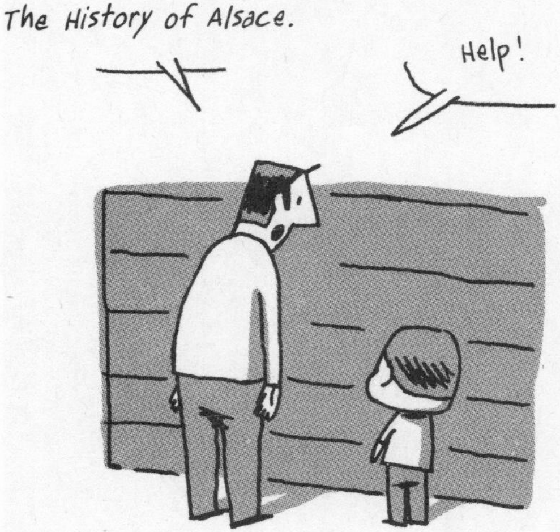
The History of Alsace.
Help!

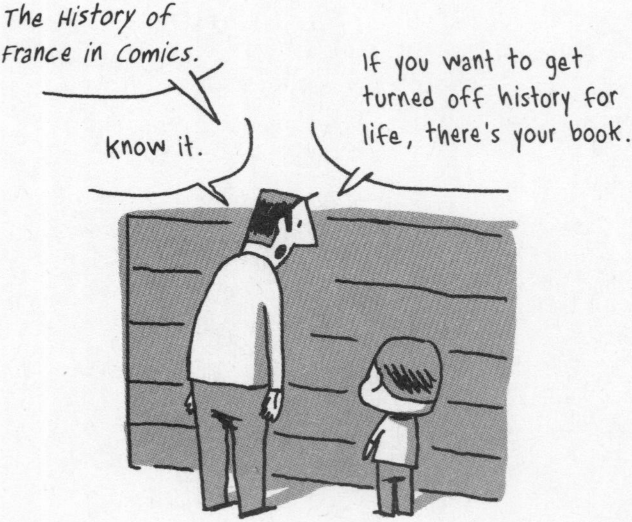
The History of France in Comics.
Know it.
If you want to get turned off history for life, there's your book.

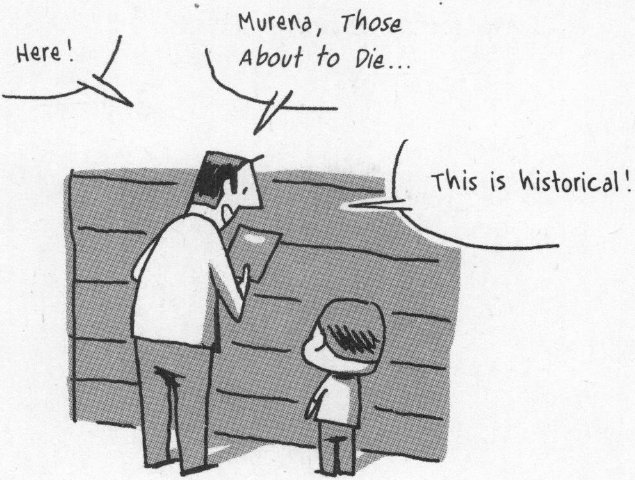
Here!
Murena, Those About to Die...
This is historical!

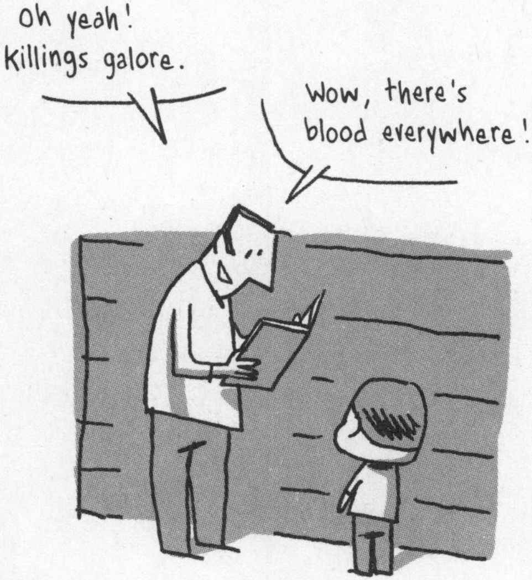
Wow, there's blood everywhere!
Oh yeah! Killings galore.

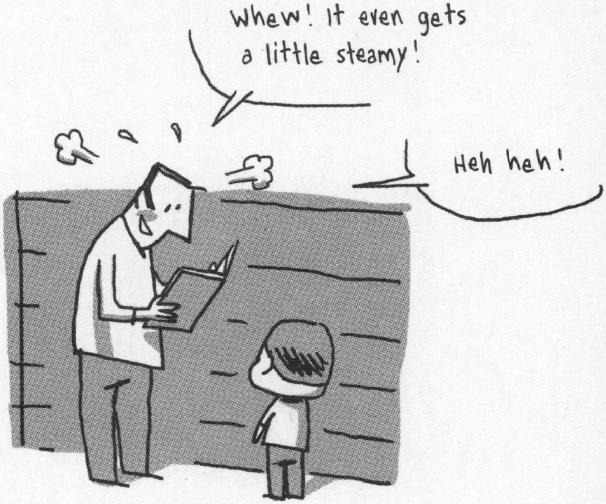
Whew! It even gets a little steamy!
Heh heh!

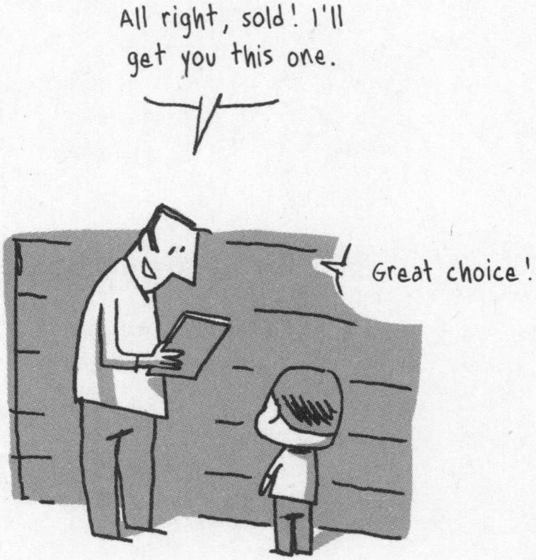
All right, sold! I'll get you this one.
Great choice!

Okay, so gladiators aren't exactly the period we were looking for, but it's roughly the Middle Ages so it should be fine.

Your teacher's gonna be thrilled!

DELISLE
2013

-The Dunce

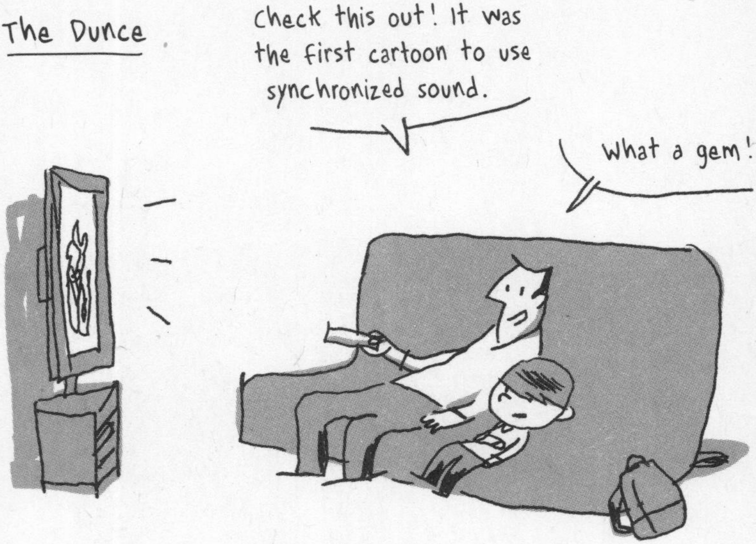
Check this out! It was the first cartoon to use synchronized sound.
What a gem!

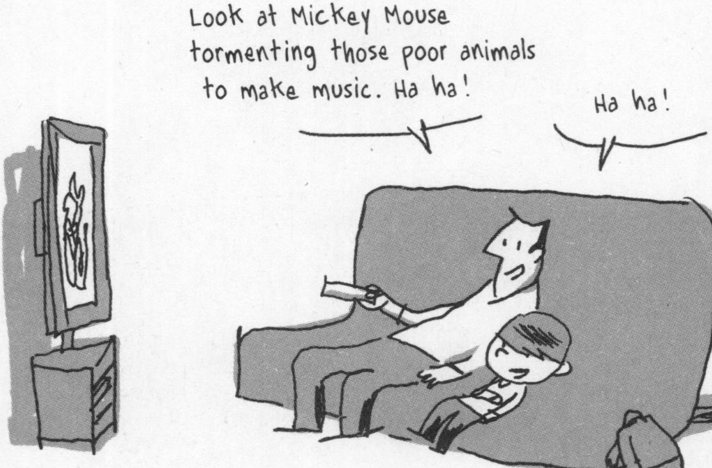
Look at Mickey Mouse tormenting those poor animals to make music. Ha ha!
Ha ha!

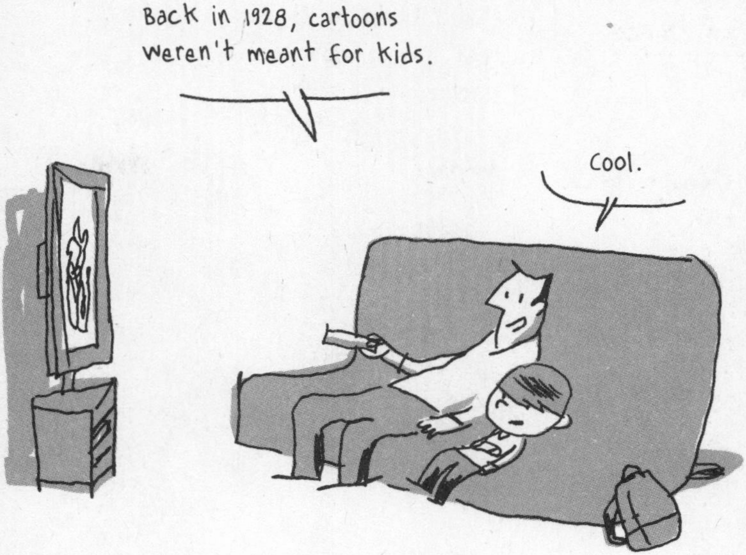
Back in 1928, cartoons weren't meant for kids.
Cool.

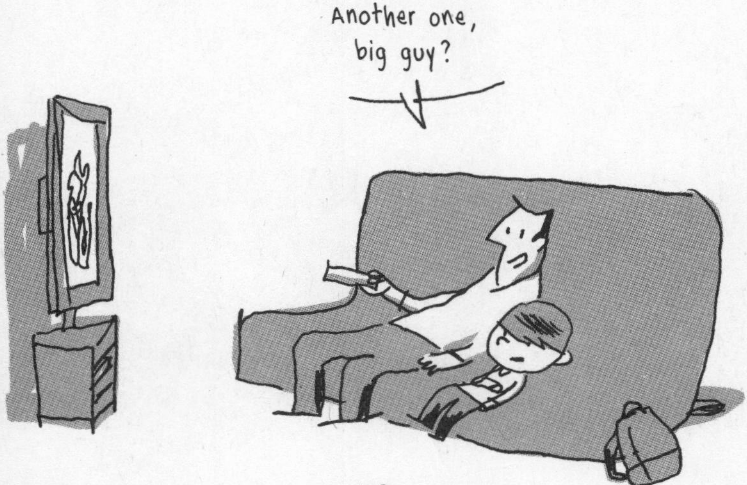
Another one, big guy?

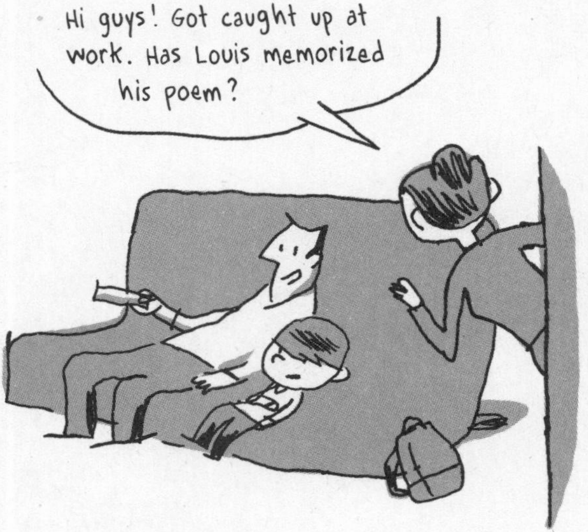
Hi guys! Got caught up at work. Has Louis memorized his poem?

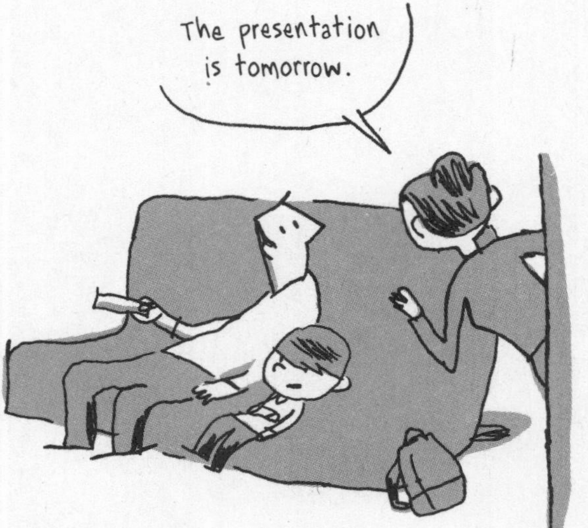
The presentation is tomorrow.

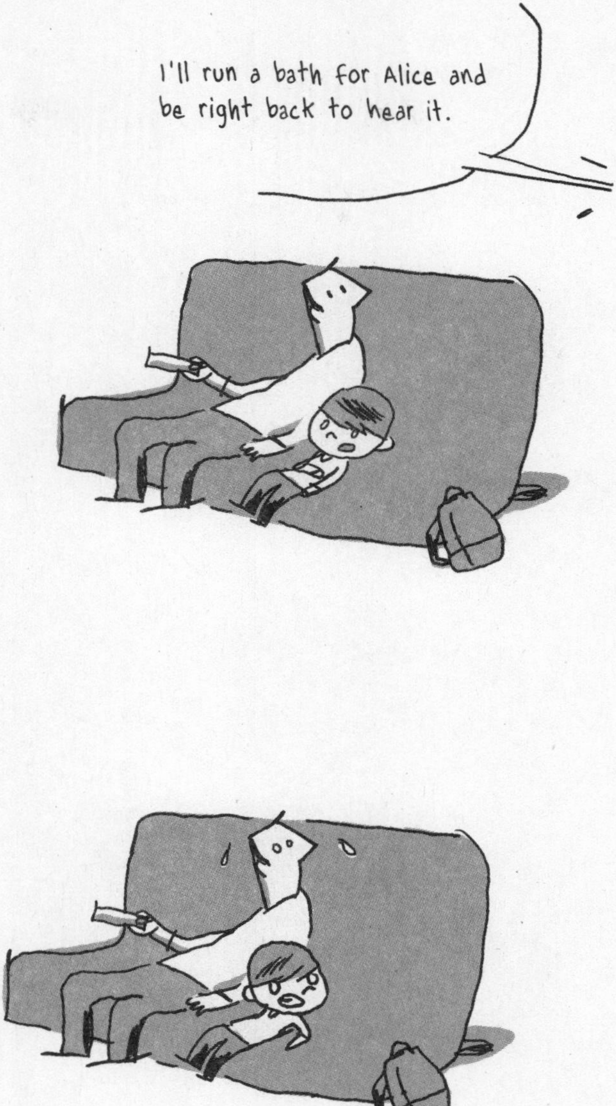
I'll run a bath for Alice and
be right back to hear it.

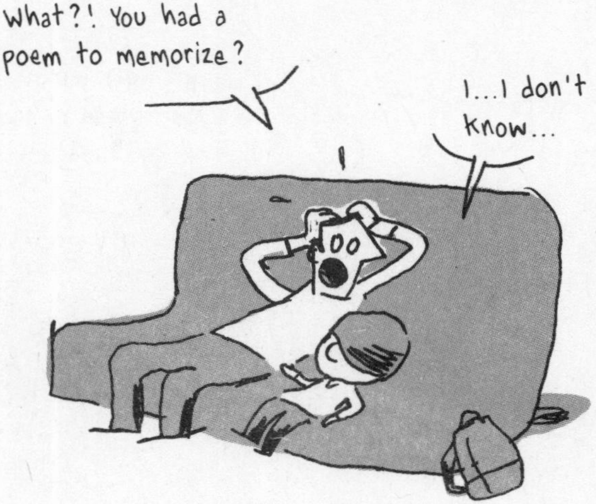
What?! You had a poem to memorize?
I...I don't know...

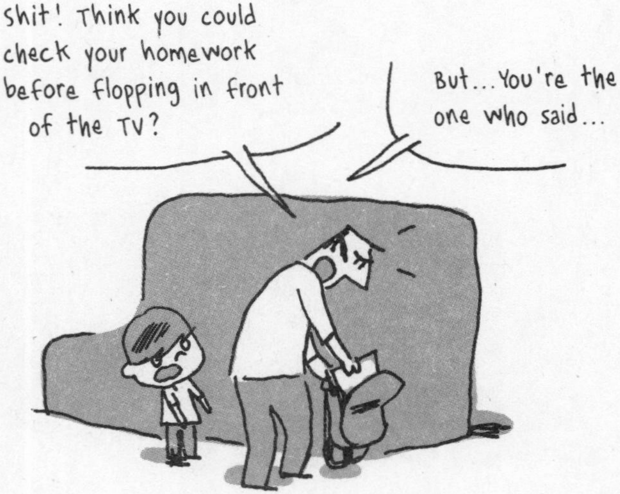
Shit! Think you could check your homework before flopping in front of the TV?
But... You're the one who said...

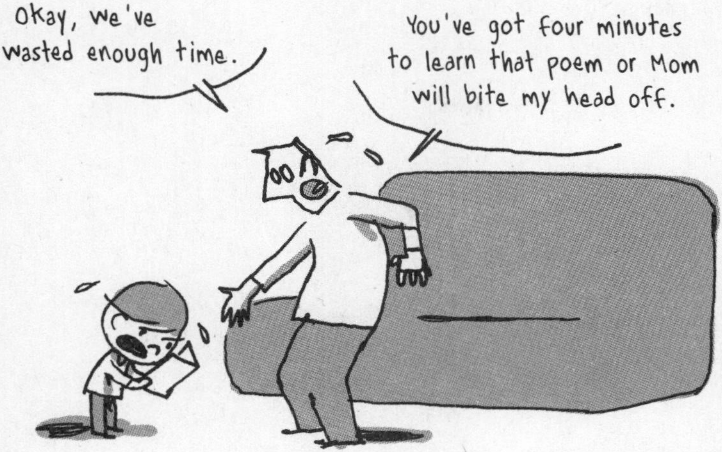
Okay, we've wasted enough time.
You've got four minutes to learn that poem or Mom will bite my head off.

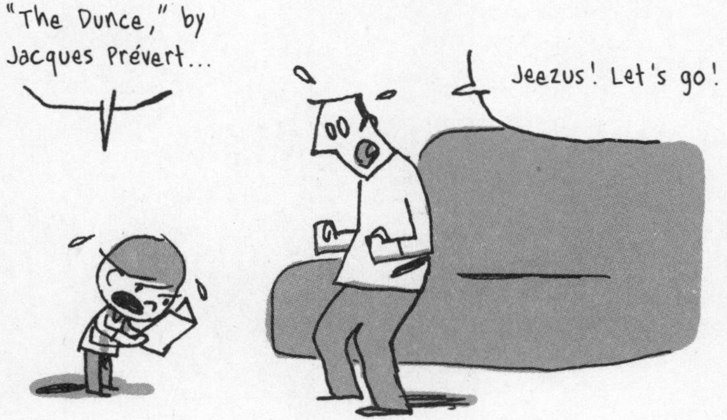
"The Dunce," by Jacques Prévert...
Jeezus! Let's go!

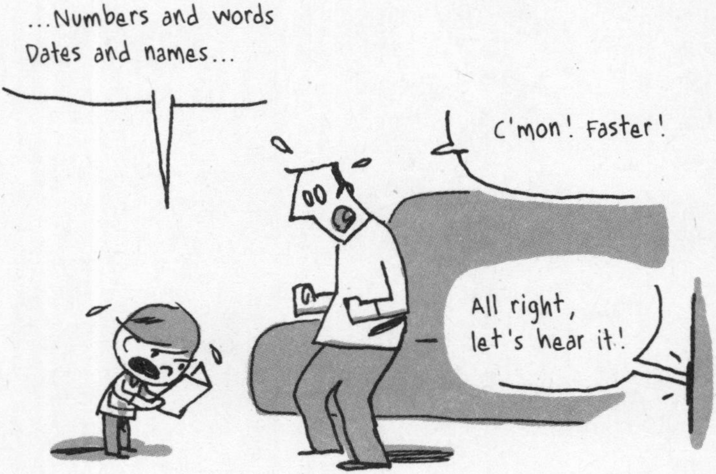
...Numbers and words
Dates and names...
C'mon! Faster!
All right, let's hear it!

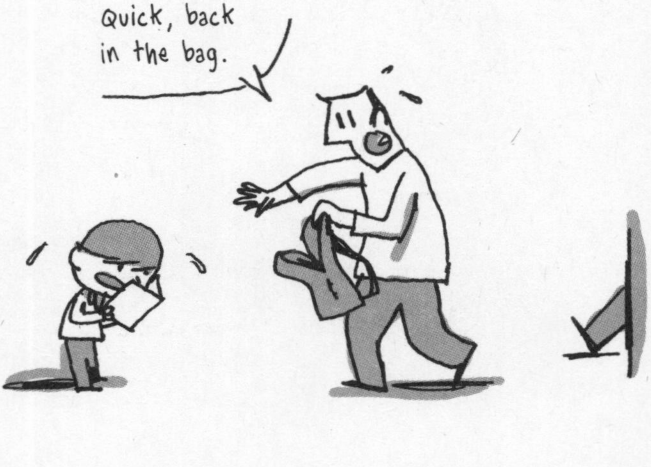
Quick, back in the bag.

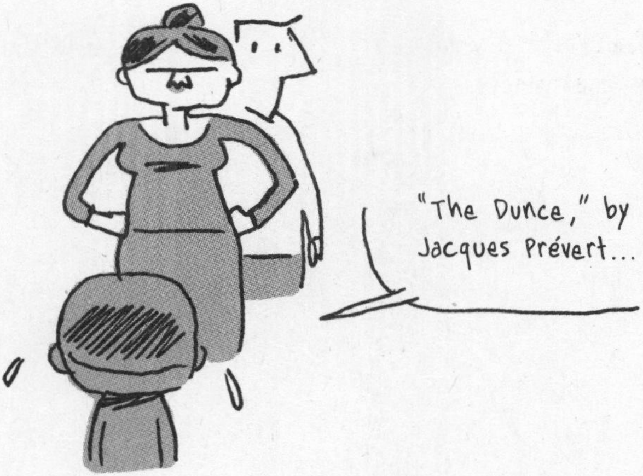
"The Dunce," by Jacques Prévert...

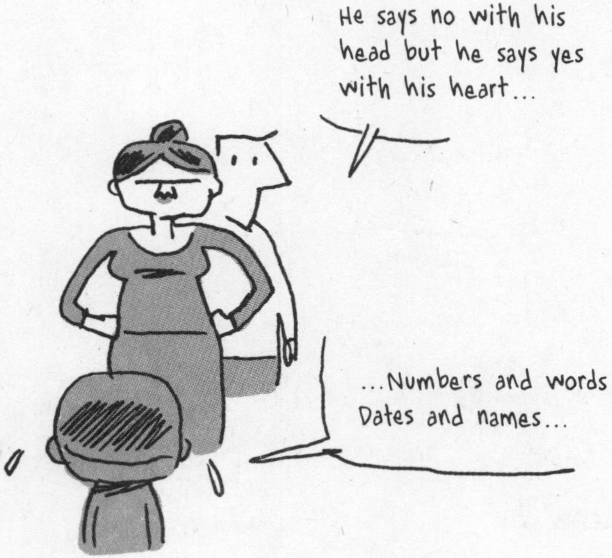
He says no with his head but he says yes with his heart...
...Numbers and words Dates and names...

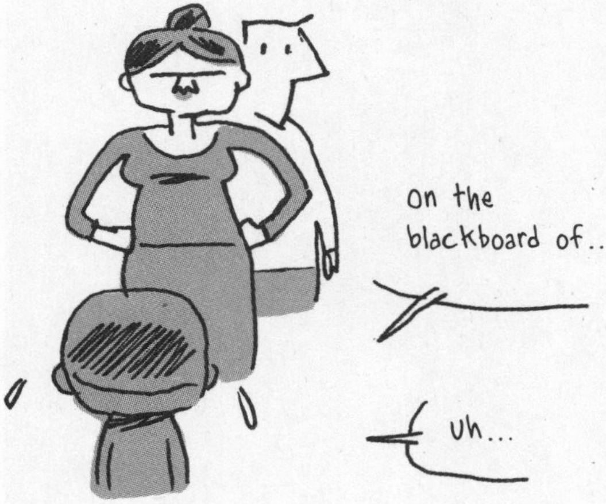
On the blackboard of...
Uh...

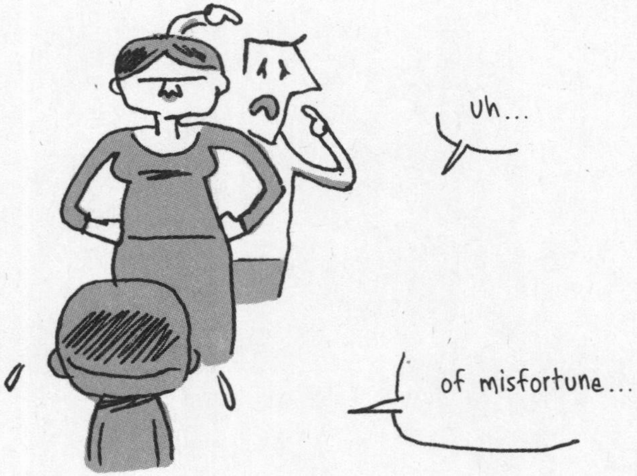
Uh...
of misfortune...

He...

draws...

He draws the
face of...

the face of...

happiness...

the face of happiness.

Fine.

That'll do.

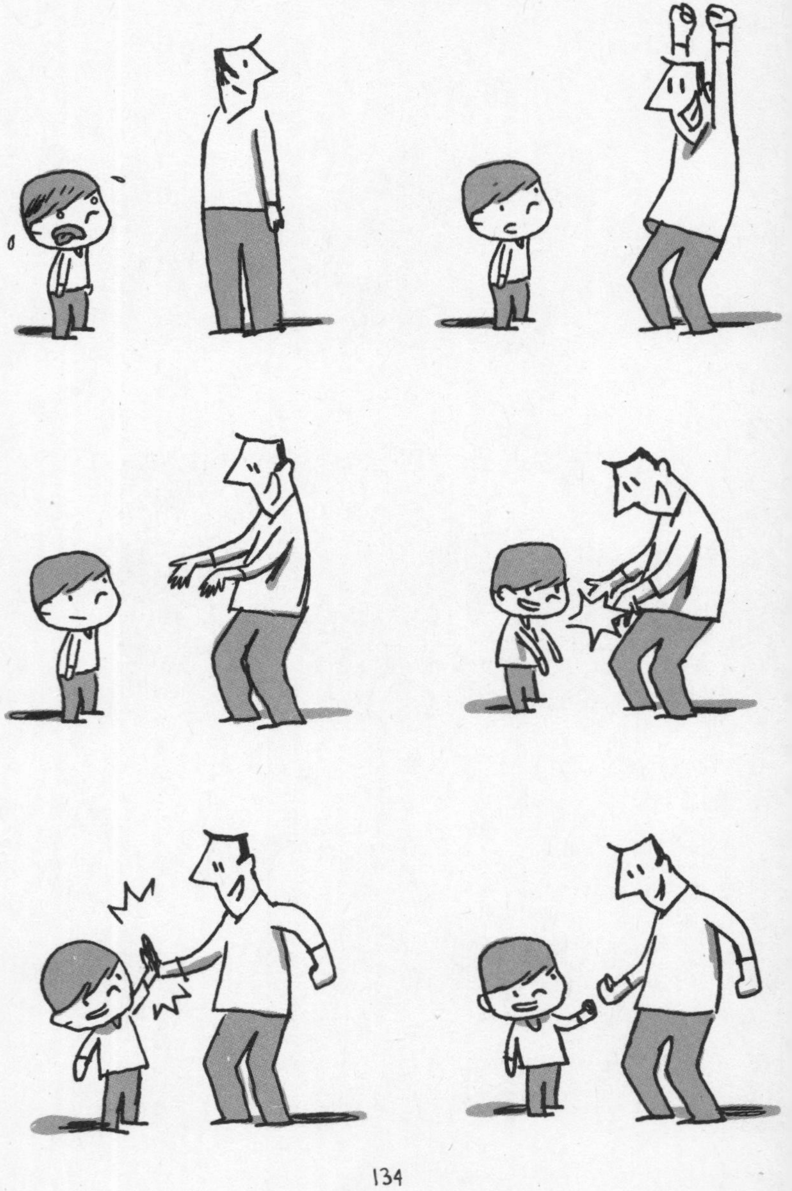

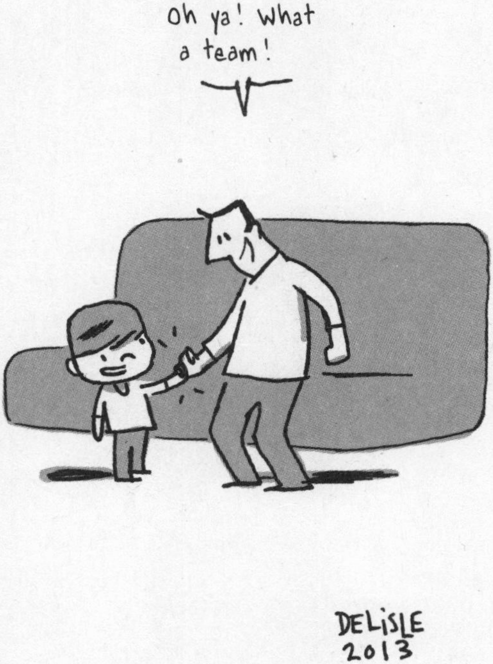
Oh ya! What a team!
DELISLE 2013

-Swimming at Reunion Island

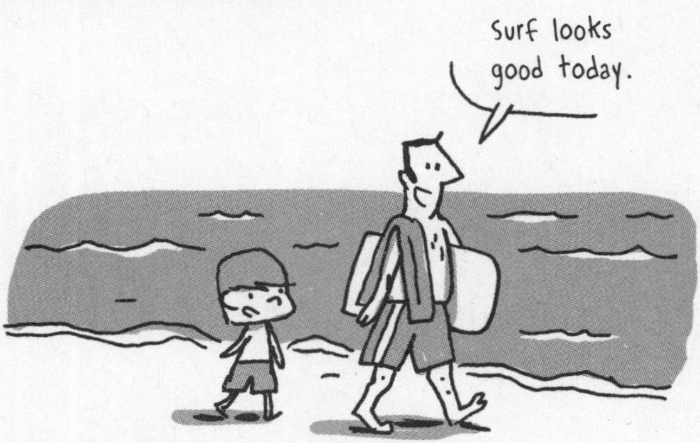
Surf looks good today.

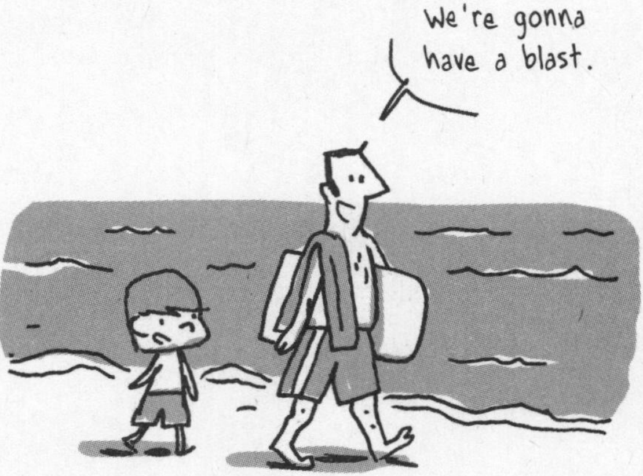
We're gonna have a blast.

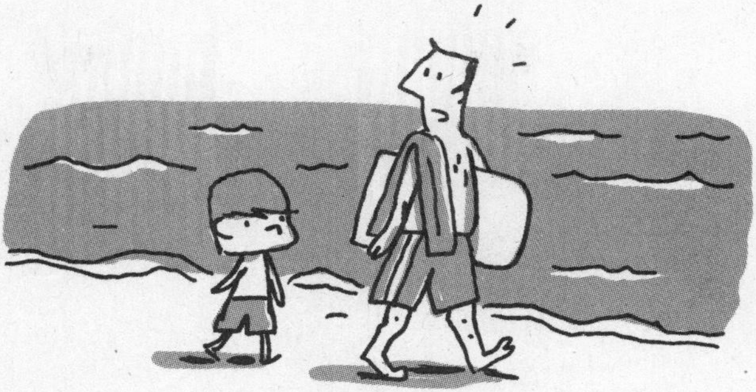

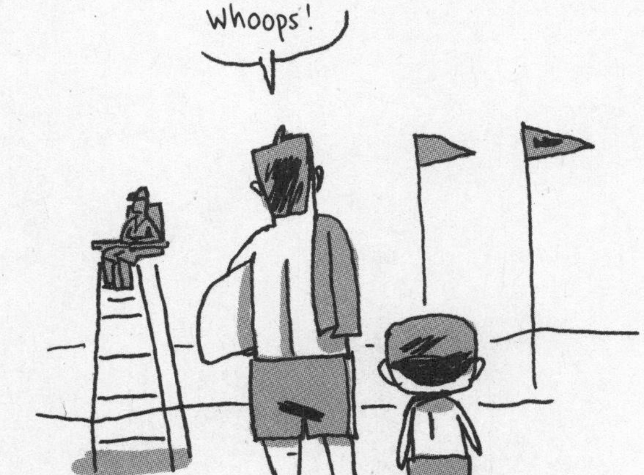
Whoops!

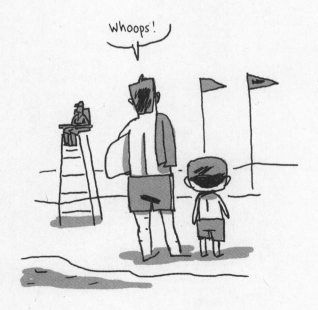

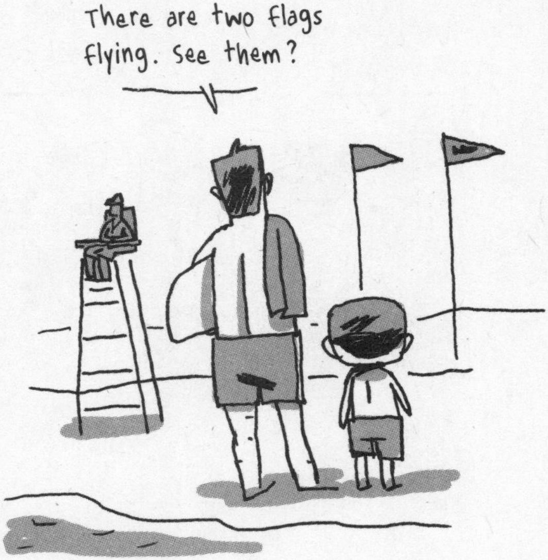
There are two flags flying. See them?

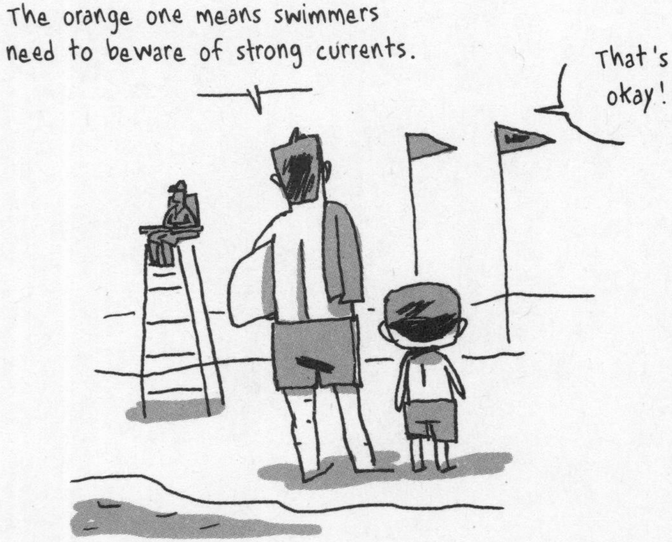
The orange one means swimmers need to beware of strong currents.
That's okay!

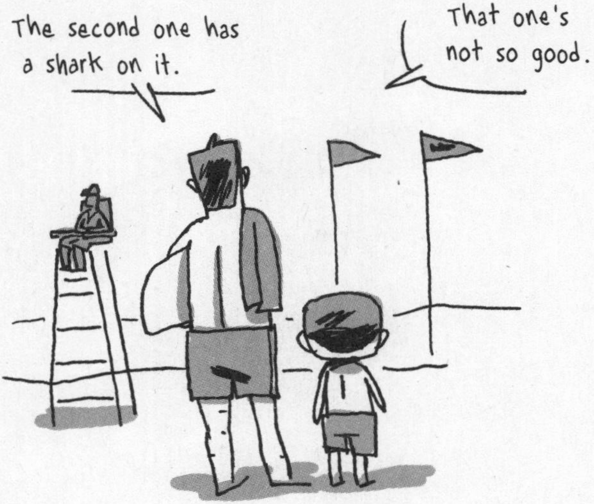
The second one has a shark on it.
That one's not so good.

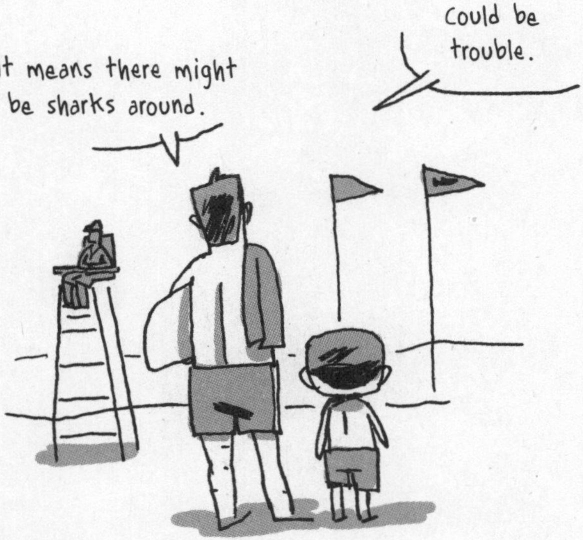
It means there might be sharks around.
Could be trouble.

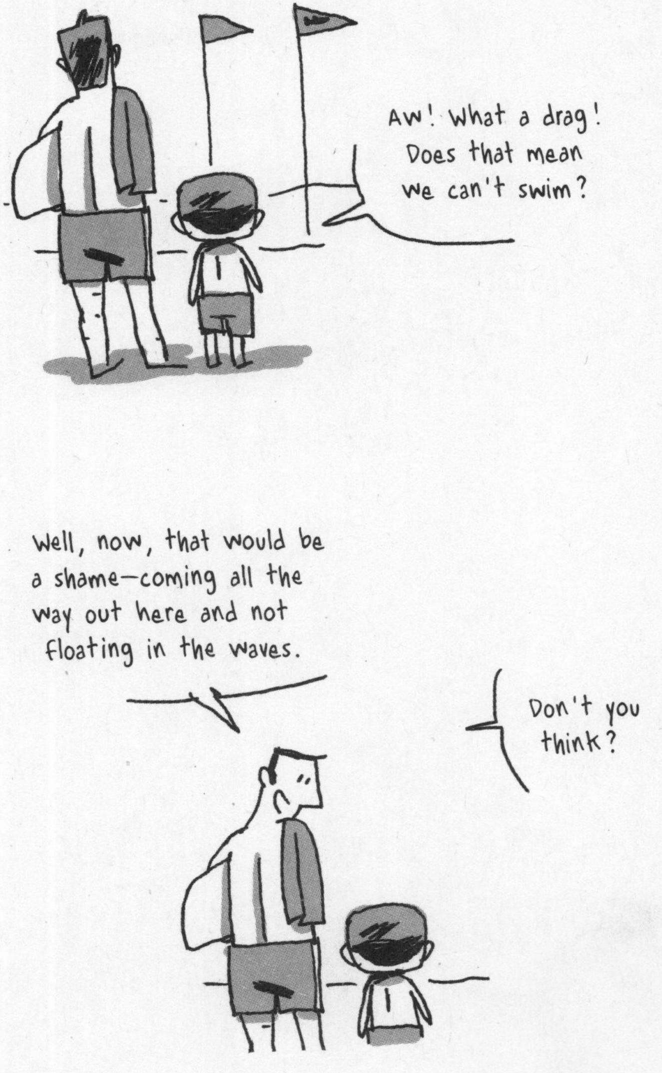
Aw! What a drag! Does that mean we can't swim?
Well, now, that would be a shame—coming all the way out here and not floating in the waves.
Don't you think?

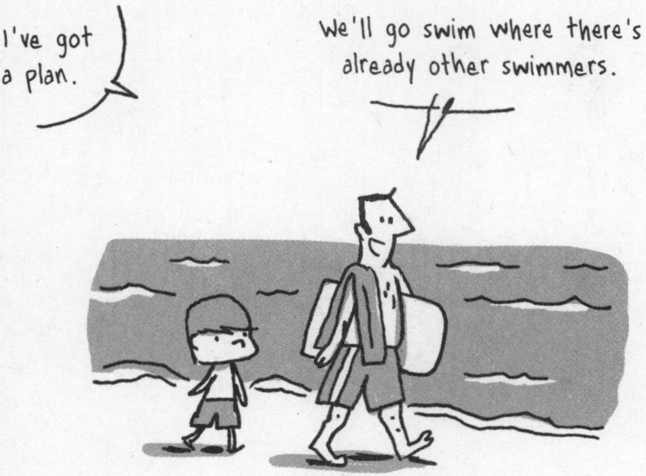
I've got a plan.
We'll go swim where there's already other swimmers.

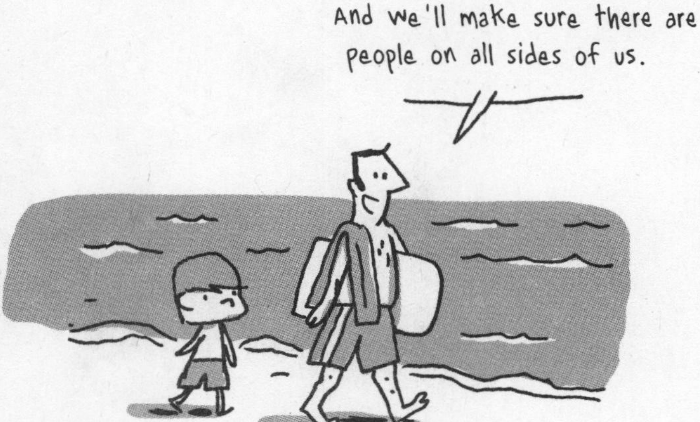
And we'll make sure there are people on all sides of us.

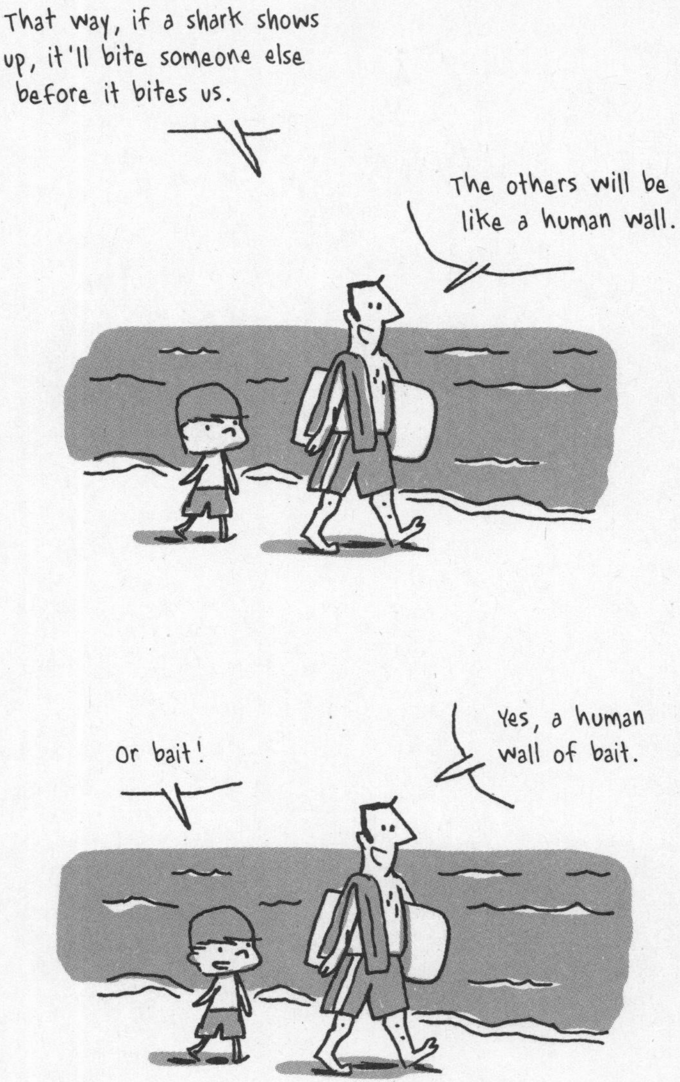
That way, if a shark shows up, it'll bite someone else before it bites us.
The others will be like a human wall.
Or bait!
Yes, a human wall of bait.

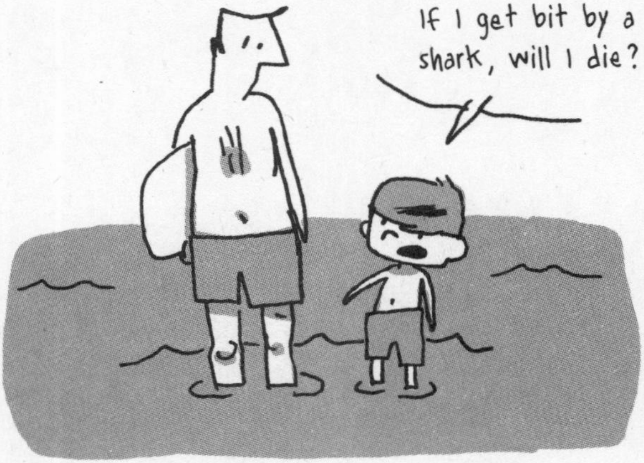
If I get bit by a shark, will I die?

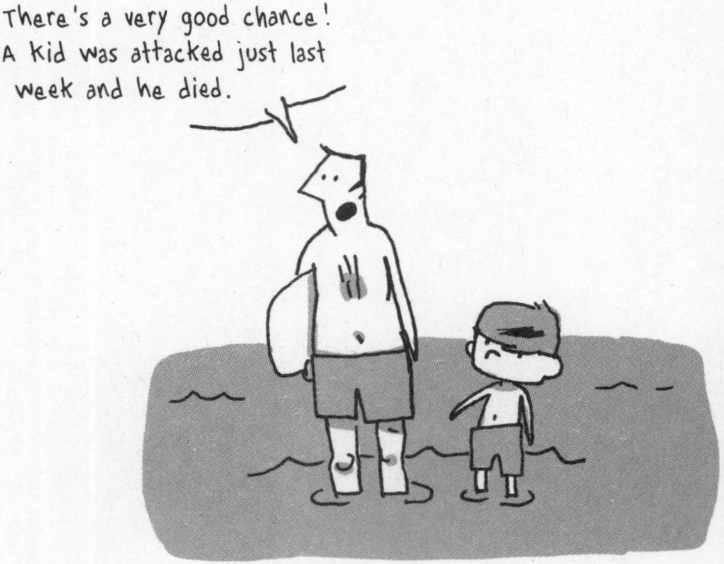
There's a very good chance! A kid was attacked just last week and he died.

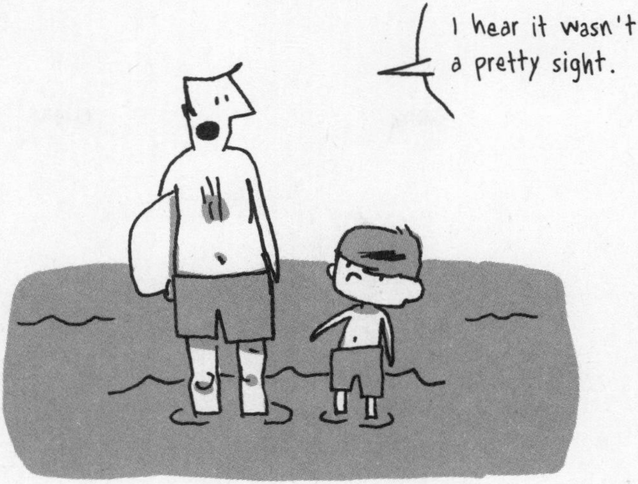
I hear it wasn't a pretty sight.

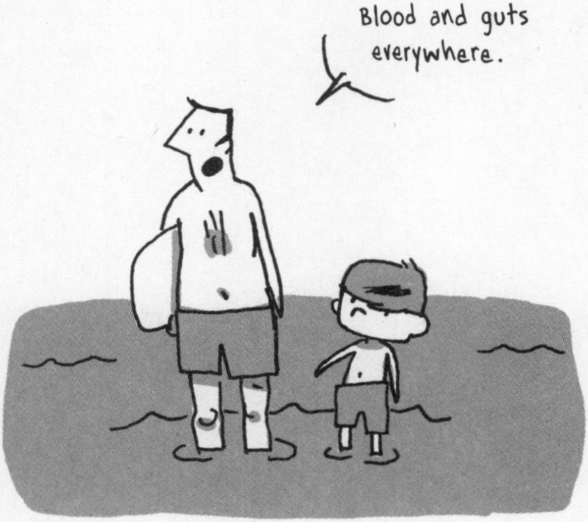
Blood and guts everywhere.

Does it hurt to die?

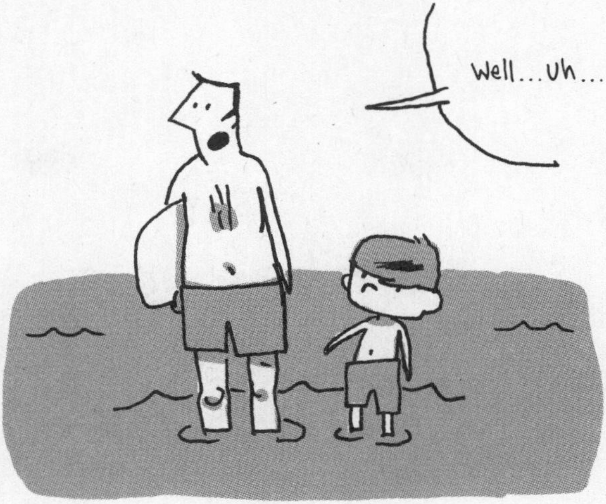
Well...uh...

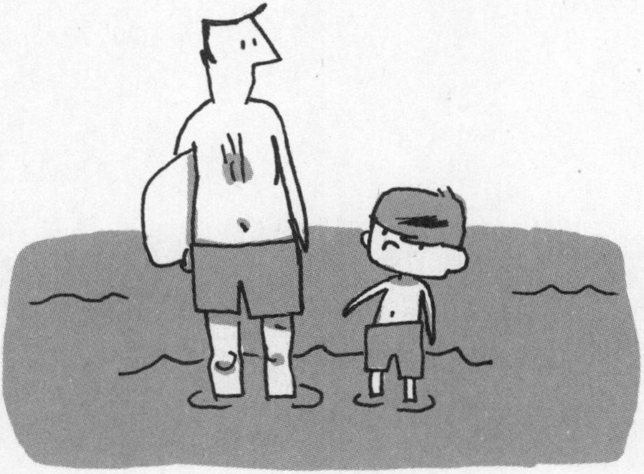

That depends...

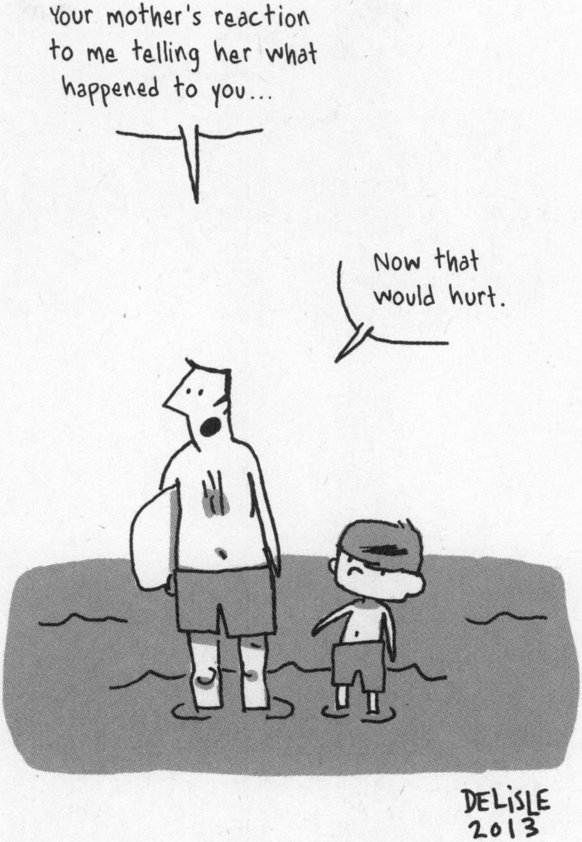
Your mother's reaction to me telling her what happened to you...
Now that would hurt.
DELISLE 2013

-The Housewarming Party

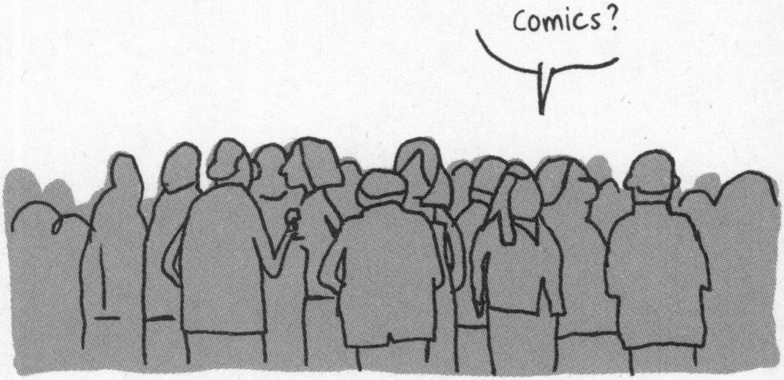
Comics?

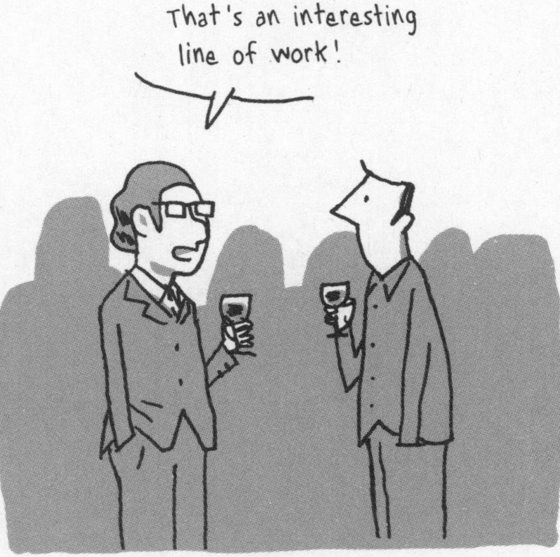
That's an interesting line of work!

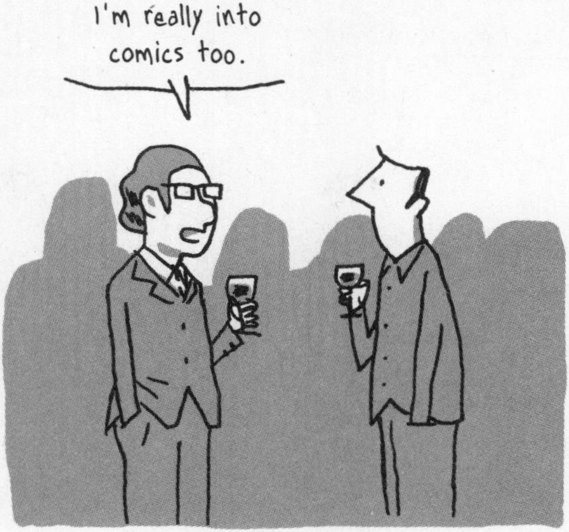
I'm really into comics too.

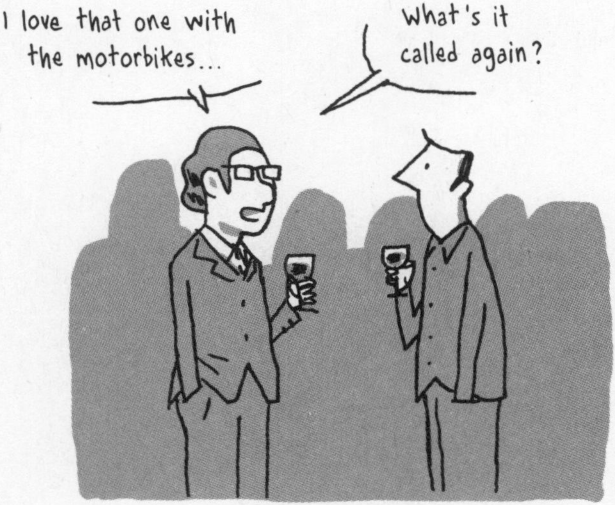
I love that one with the motorbikes...
What's it called again?

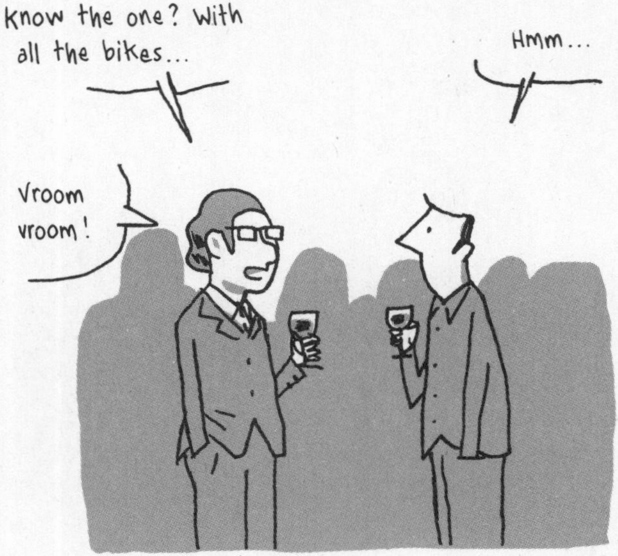
Know the one? With all the bikes...
Hmm...
Vroom vroom!

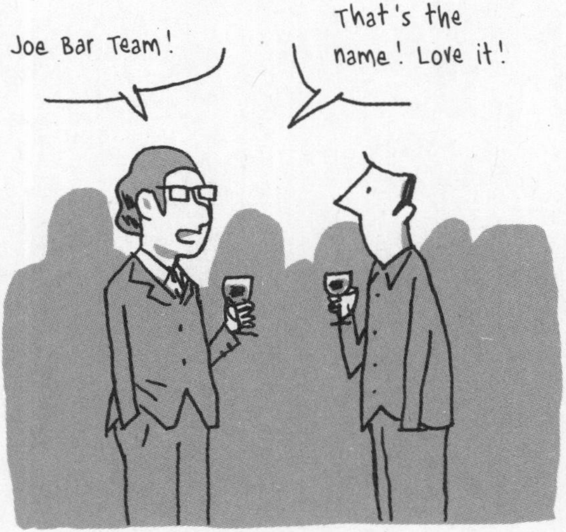
Joe Bar Team!
That's the name! Love it!

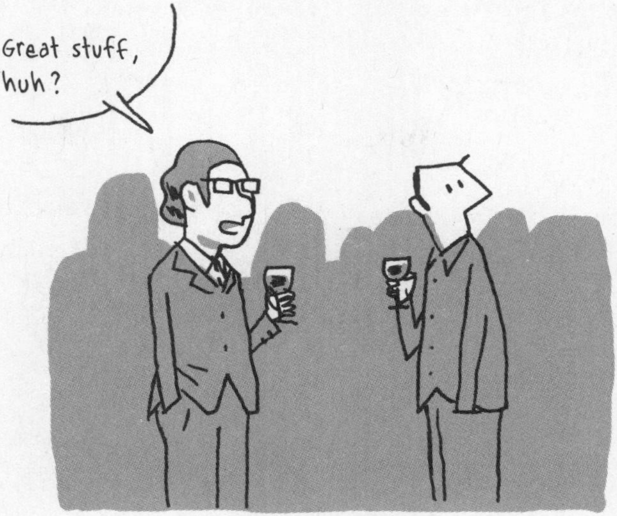
Great stuff,
huh?

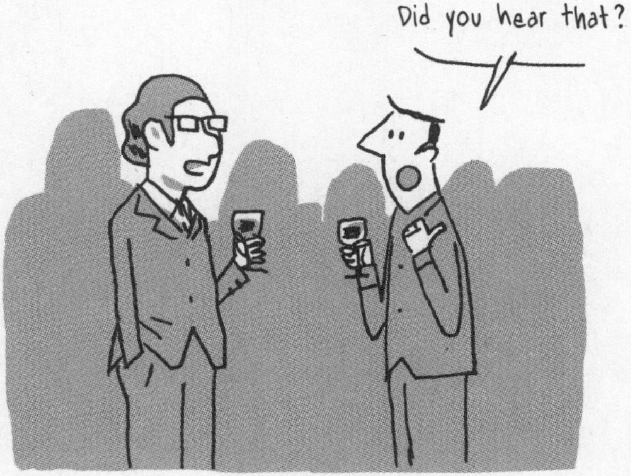
Did you hear that?

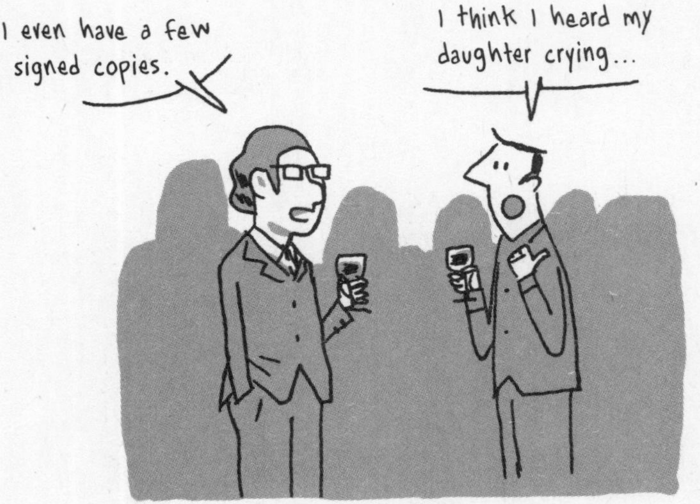
I even have a few signed copies.
I think I heard my daughter crying...

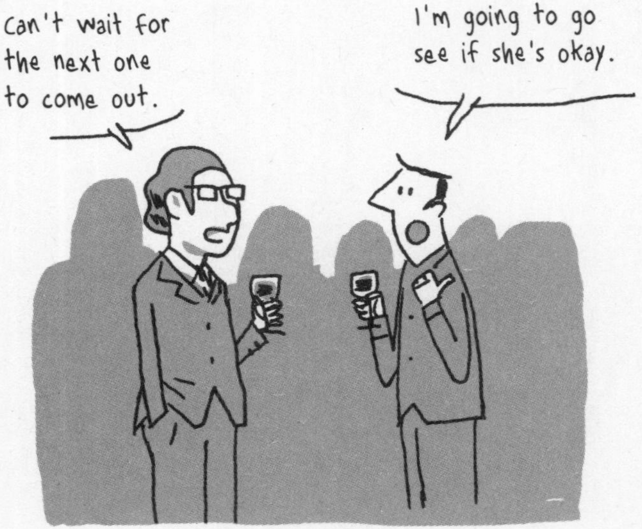
Can't wait for the next one to come out.
I'm going to go see if she's okay.

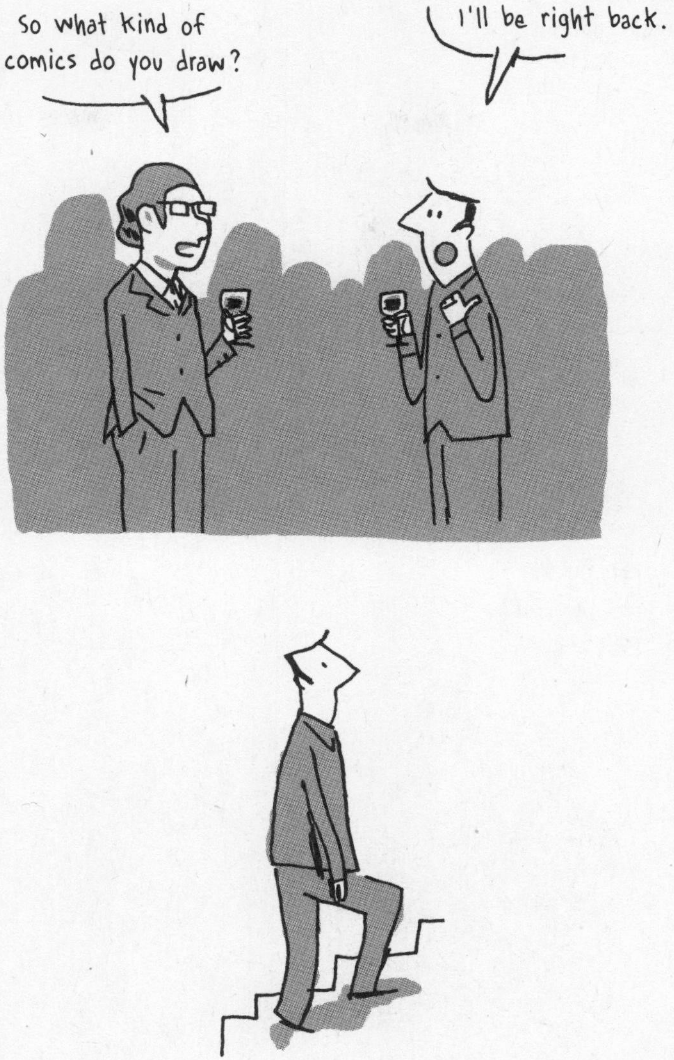
So what kind of comics do you draw?
I'll be right back.

I think we need to go now. She's getting a bit tired.

oh!

I'm not tired!

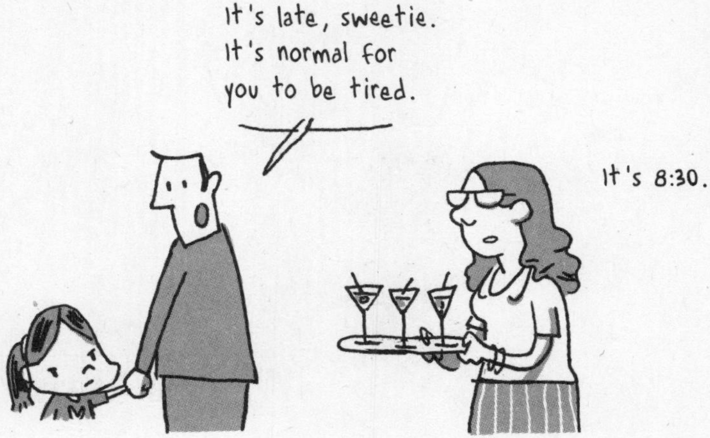
It's late, sweetie. It's normal for you to be tired.
It's 8:30.

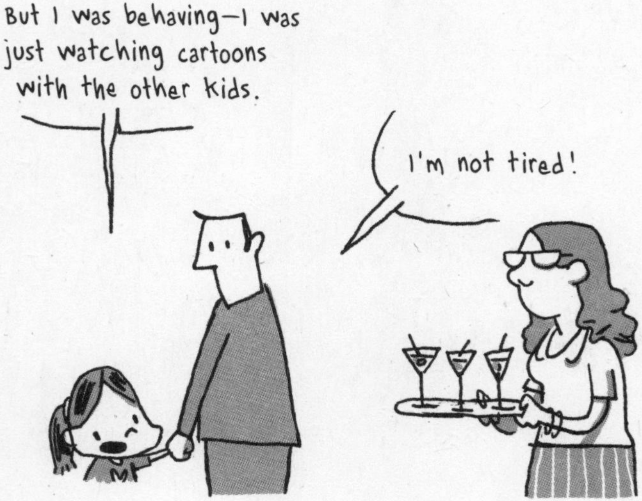
But I was behaving—I was just watching cartoons with the other kids.
I'm not tired!

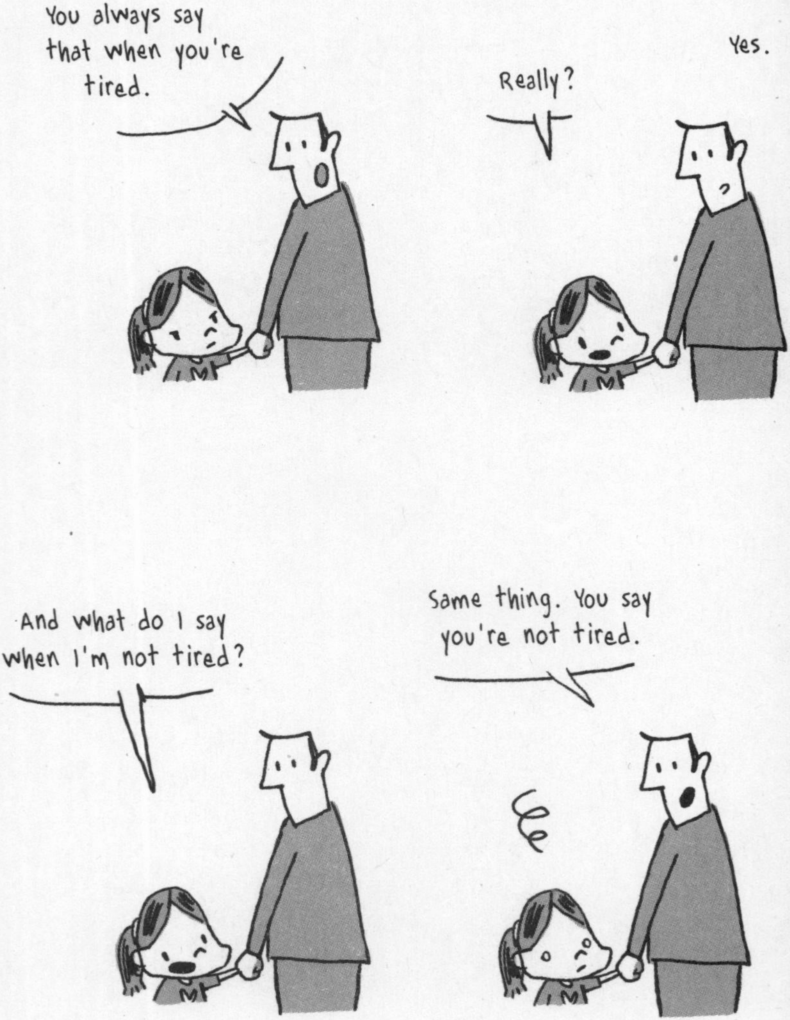
You always say that when you're tired.
Really?
Yes.
And what do I say when I'm not tired?
Same thing. You say you're not tired.

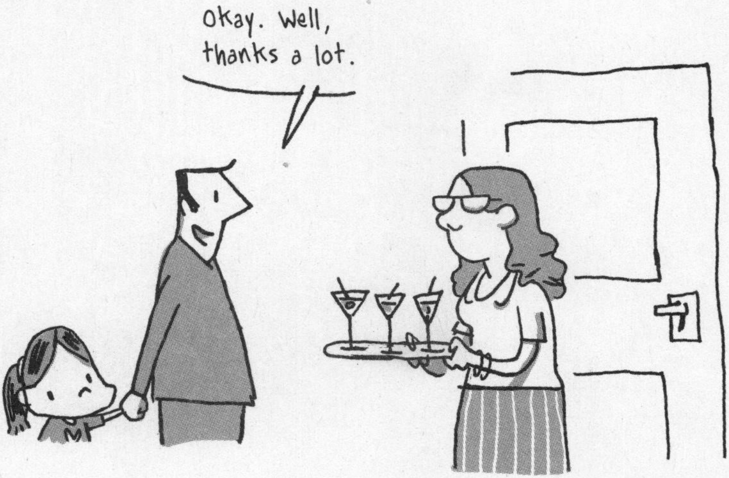
Okay. Well, thanks a lot.

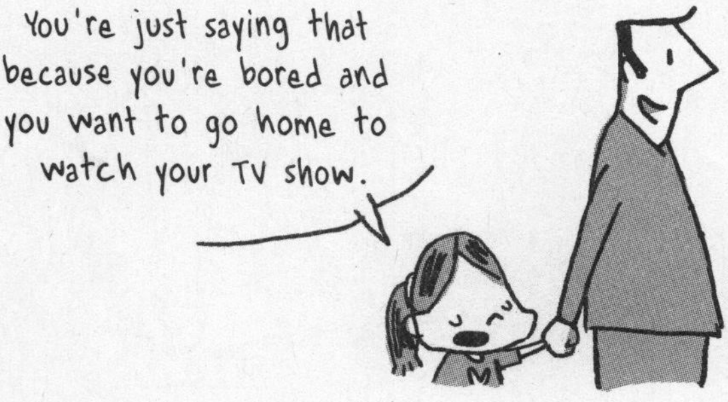
You're just saying that because you're bored and you want to go home to watch your TV show.

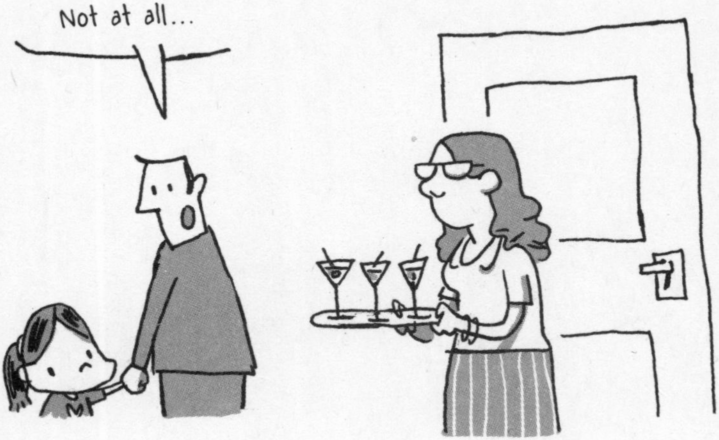
Not at all...

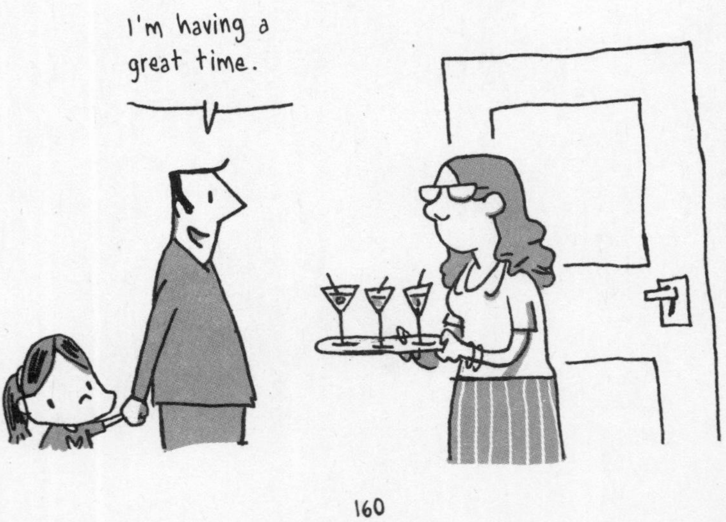
I'm having a great time.

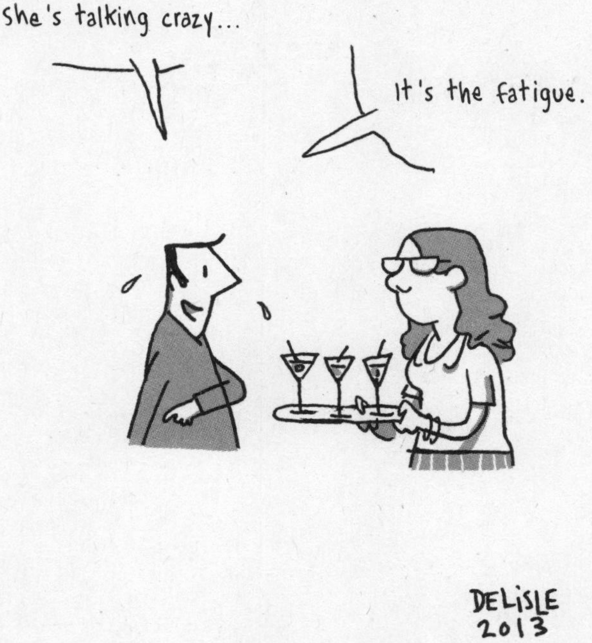
She's talking crazy...
It's the fatigue.
DELISLE
2013

-Overweight

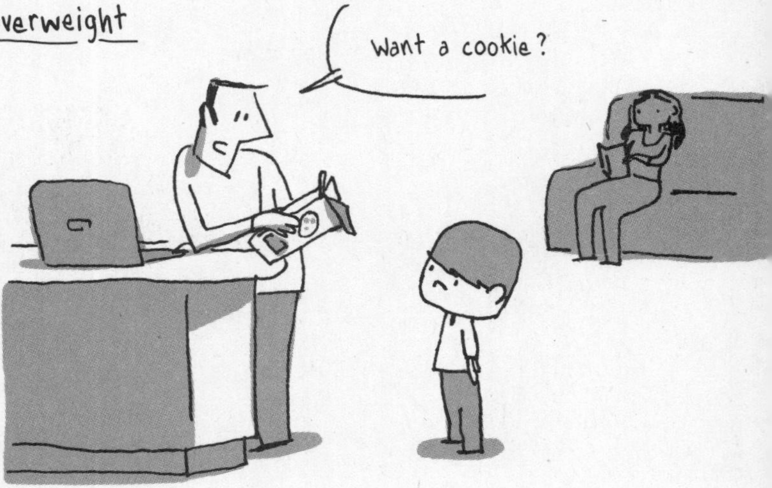
Want a cookie?

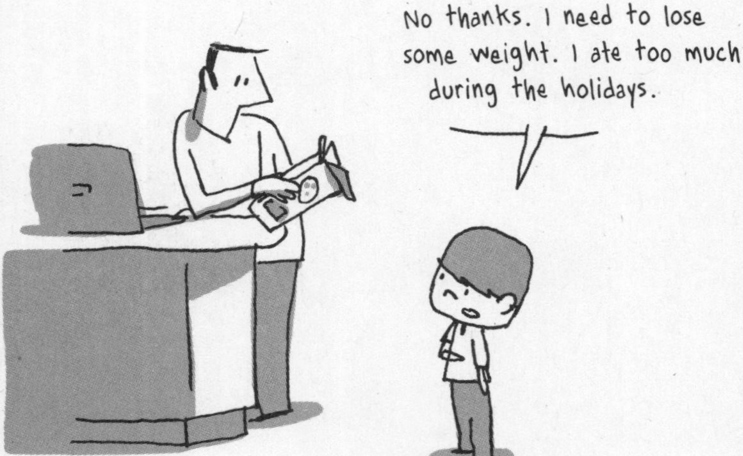
No thanks. I need to lose some weight. I ate too much during the holidays.

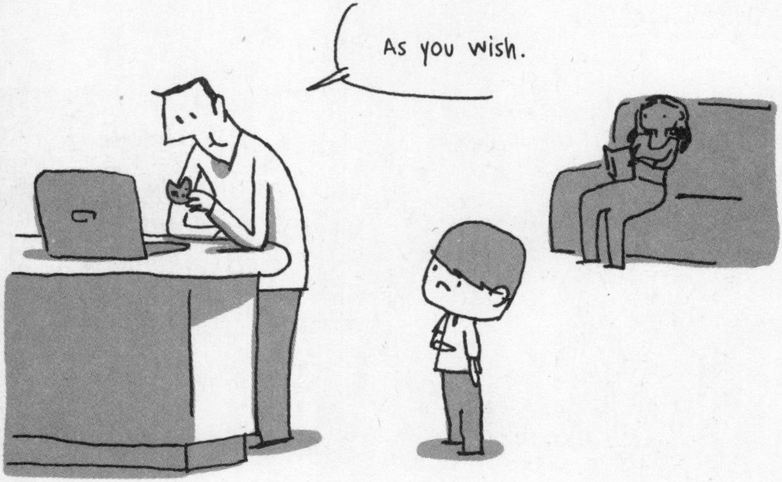
As you wish.

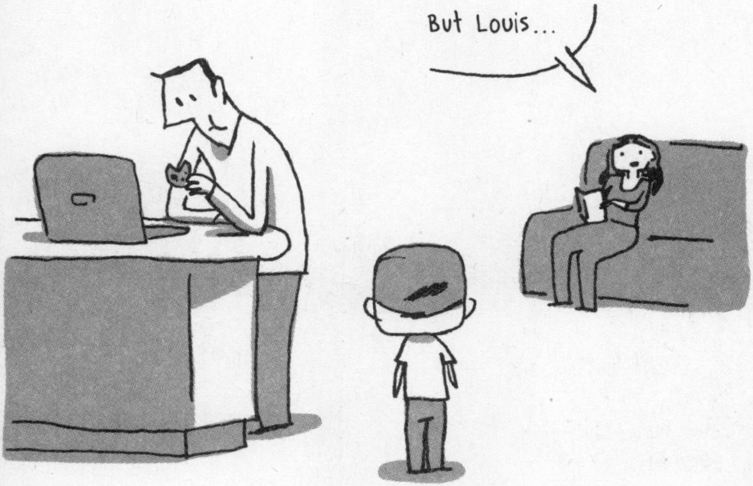
But Louis...

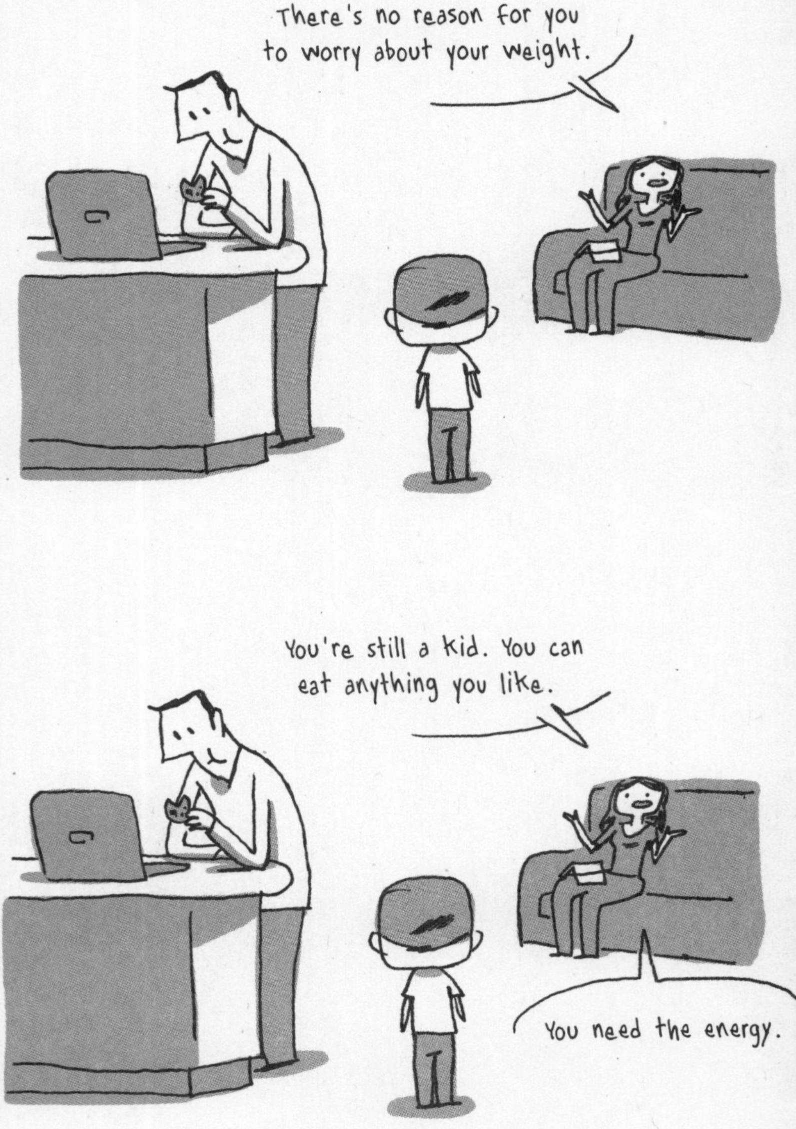
There's no reason for you to worry about your weight.
You're still a kid. You can eat anything you like.
You need the energy.

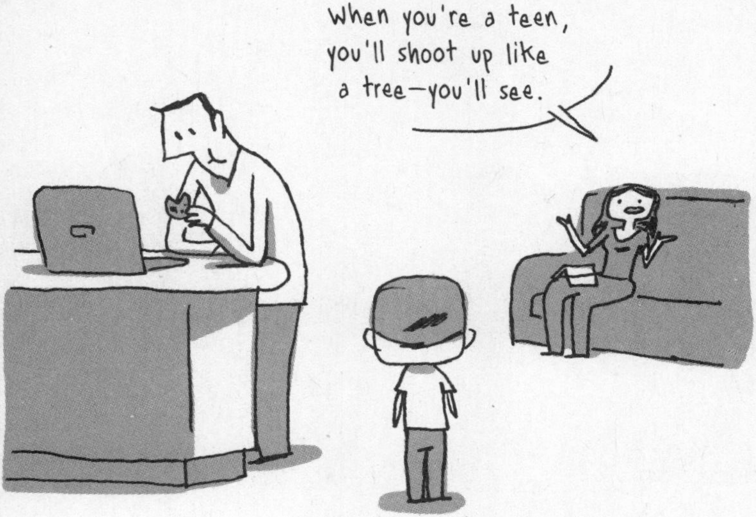
When you're a teen, you'll shoot up like a tree—you'll see.

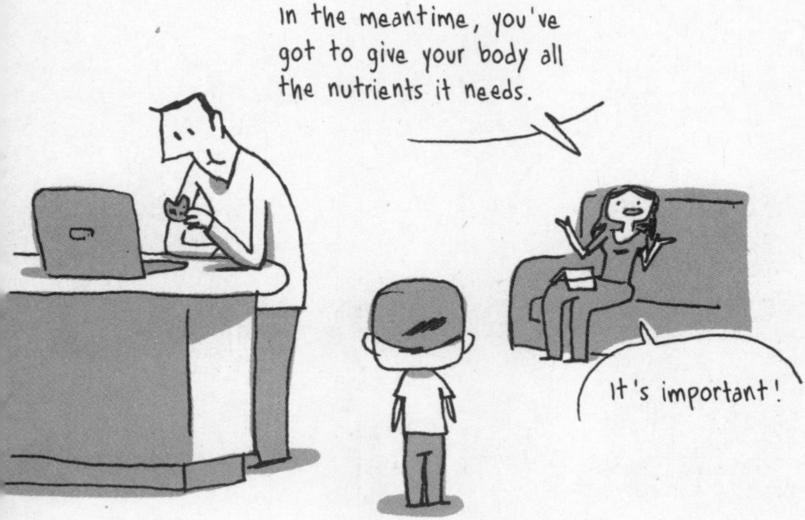
In the meantime, you've got to give your body all the nutrients it needs.
It's important!

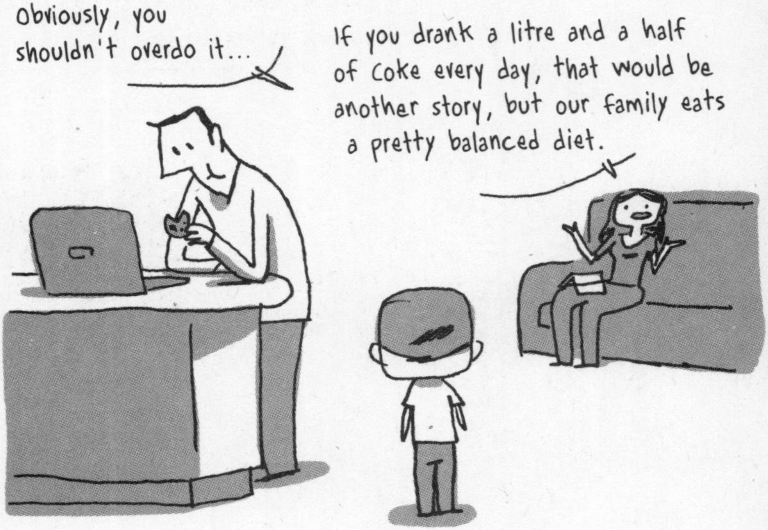
Obviously, you shouldn't overdo it...
If you drank a litre and a half of Coke every day, that would be another story, but our family eats a pretty balanced diet.

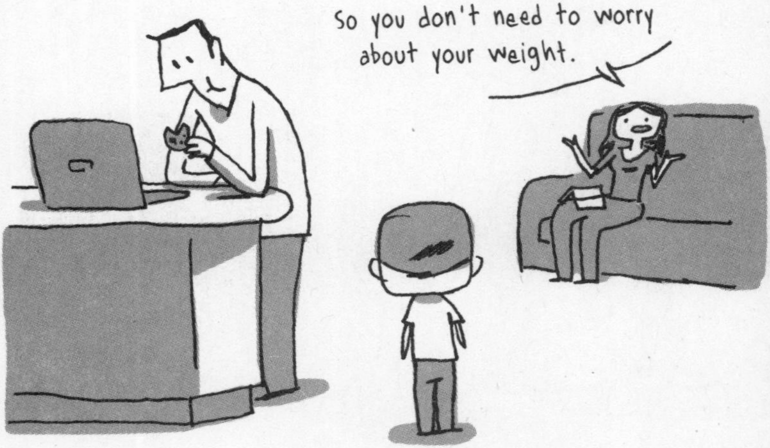
So you don't need to worry about your weight.

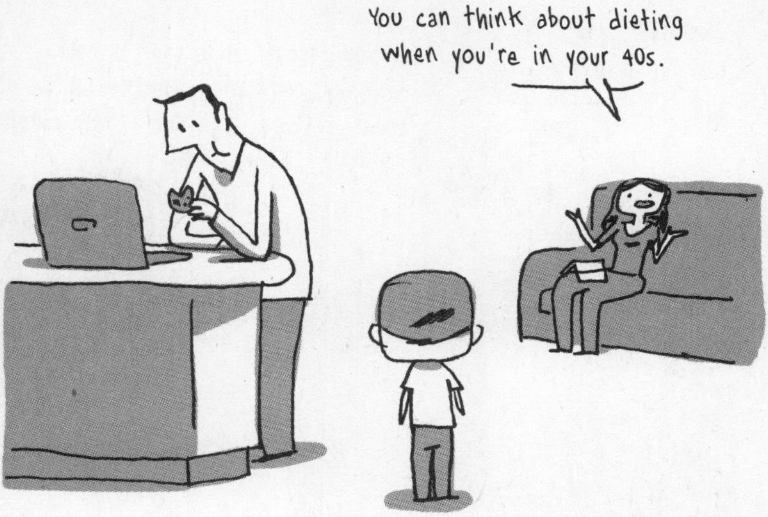
You can think about dieting when you're in your 40s.

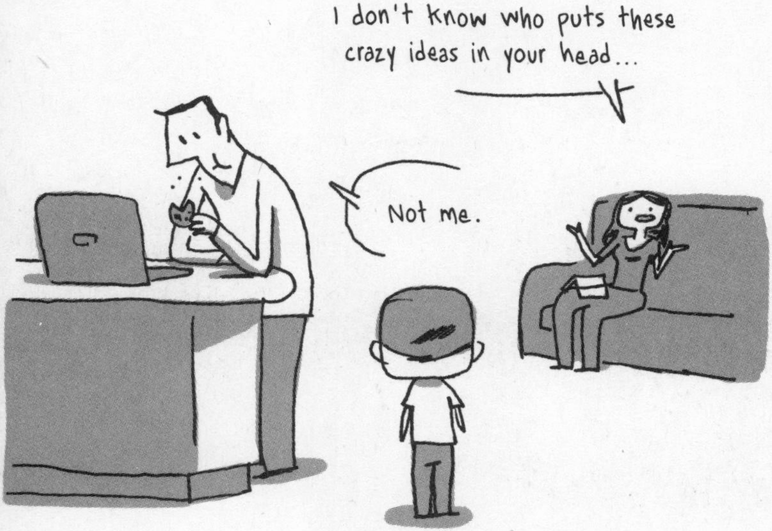
I don't know who puts these crazy ideas in your head...
Not me.

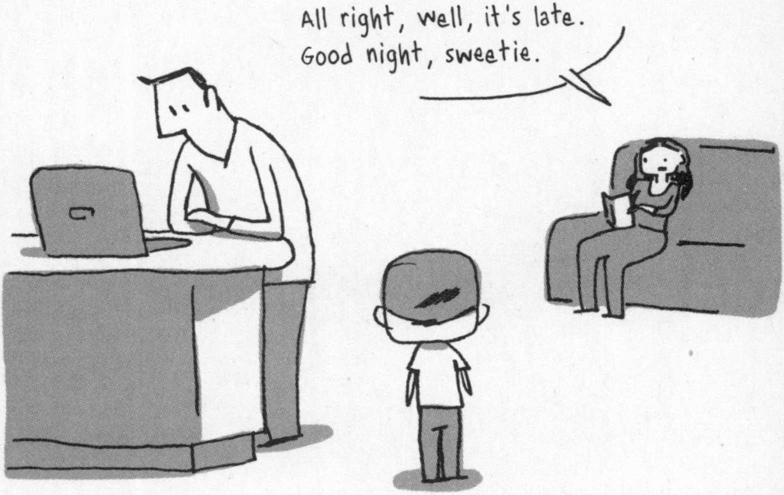
All right, well, it's late. Good night, sweetie.

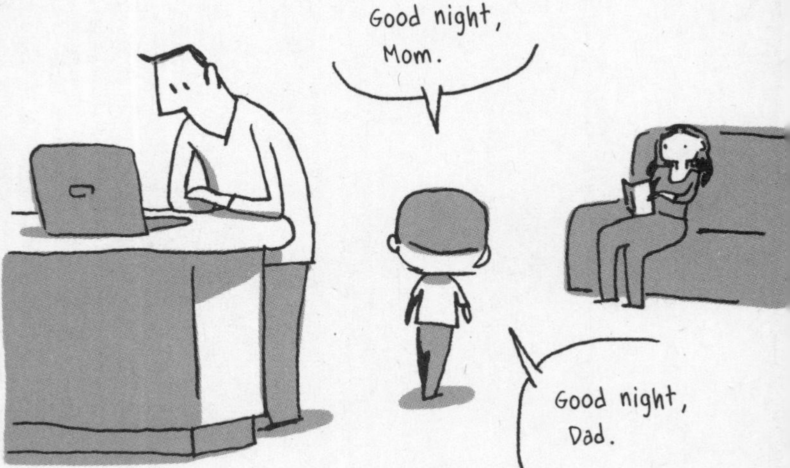
Good night, Mom.
Good night, Dad.

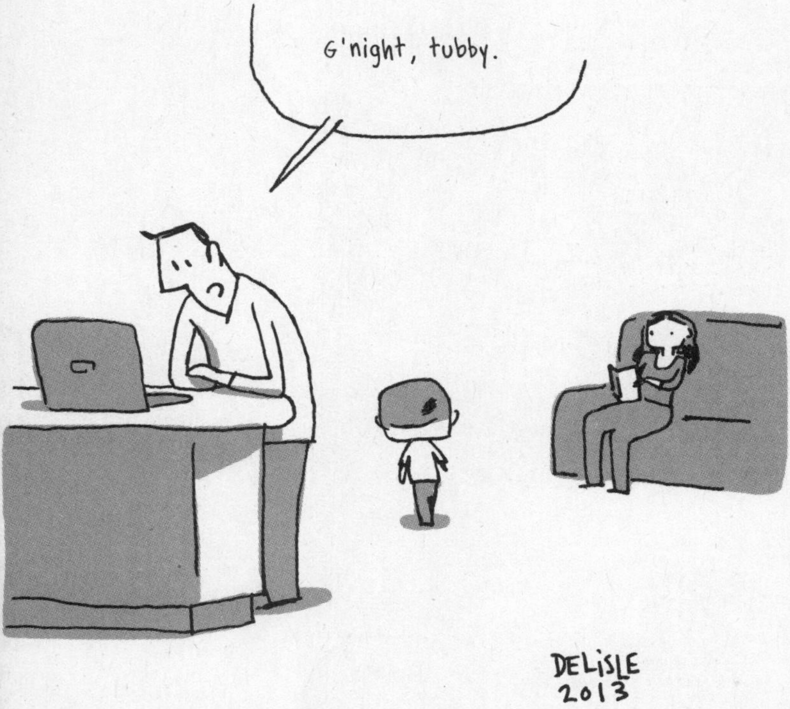
G'night, tubby.
DELISLE
2013

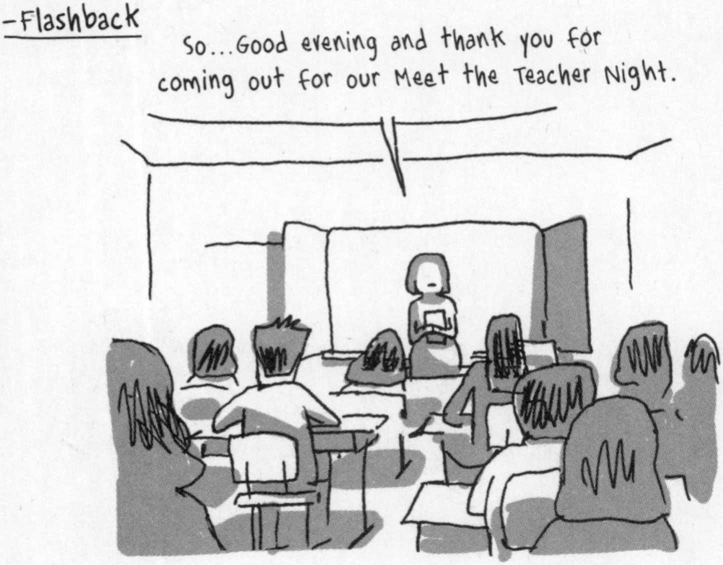
-Flashback
So...Good evening and thank you for coming out for our Meet the Teacher Night.

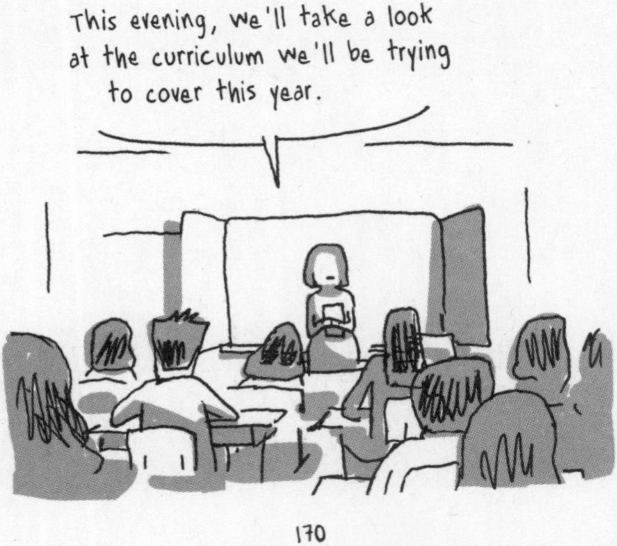
This evening, we'll take a look at the curriculum we'll be trying to cover this year.

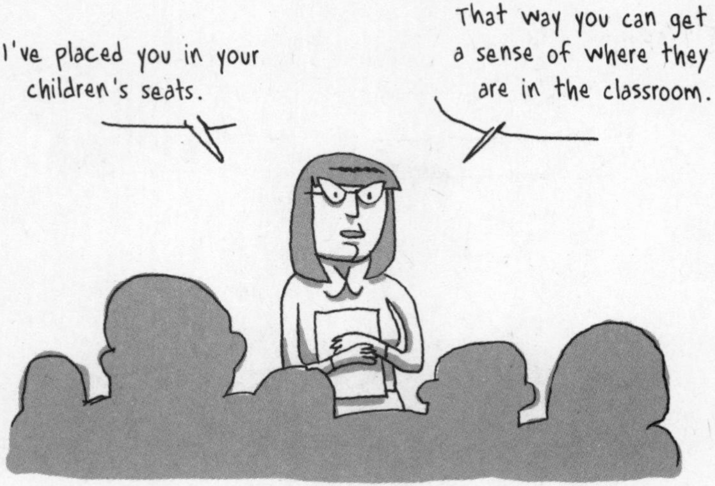
I've placed you in your children's seats.
That way you can get a sense of where they are in the classroom.

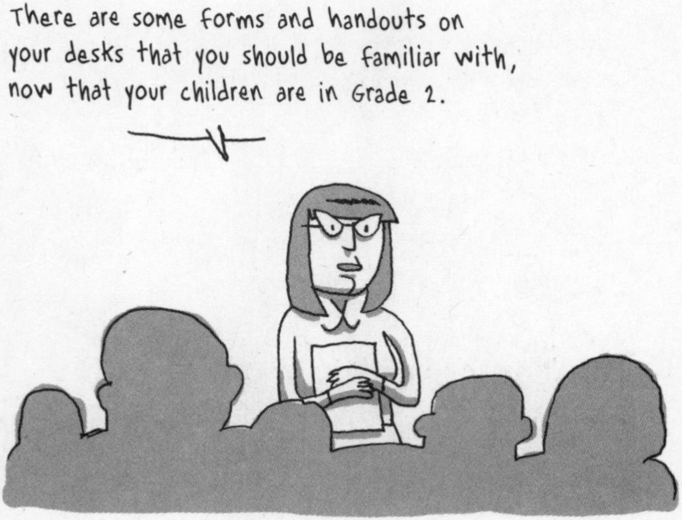
There are some forms and handouts on your desks that you should be familiar with, now that your children are in Grade 2.

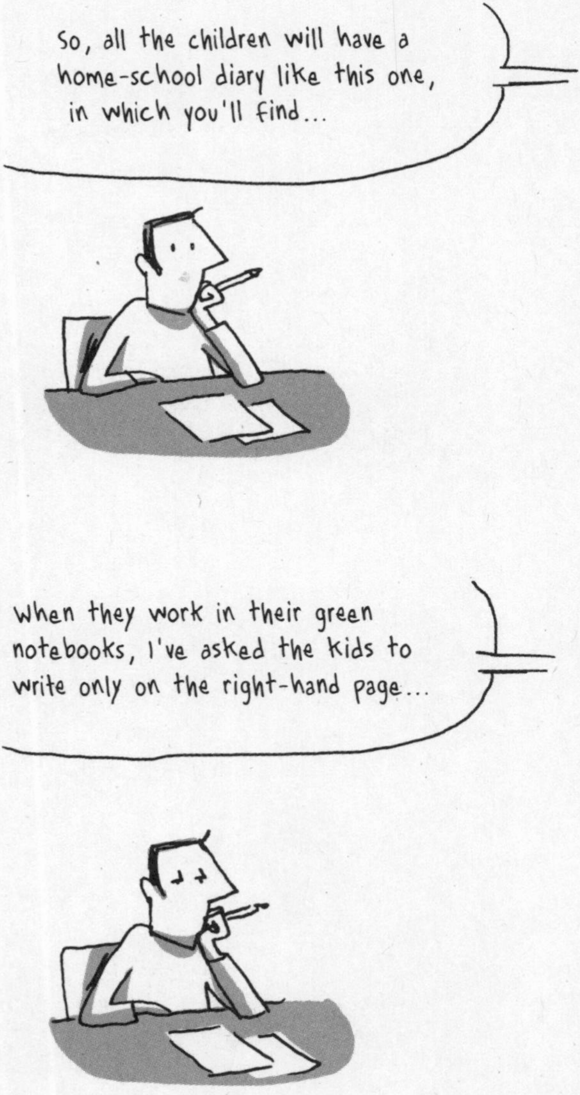
So, all the children will have a home-school diary like this one, in which you'll find...
When they work in their green notebooks, I've asked the kids to write only on the right-hand page...

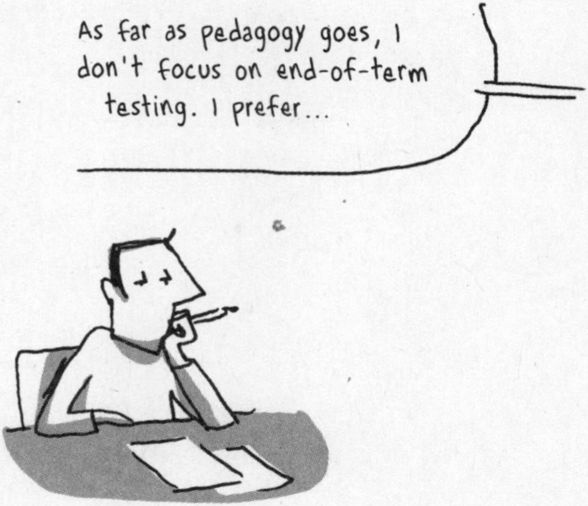
As far as pedagogy goes, I don't focus on end-of-term testing. I prefer...

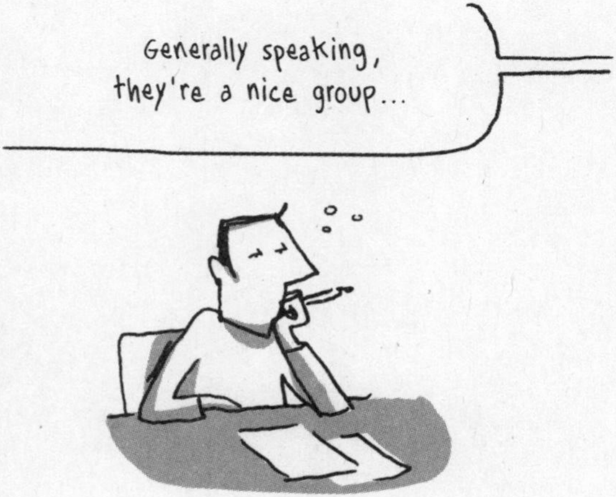
Generally speaking, they're a nice group...

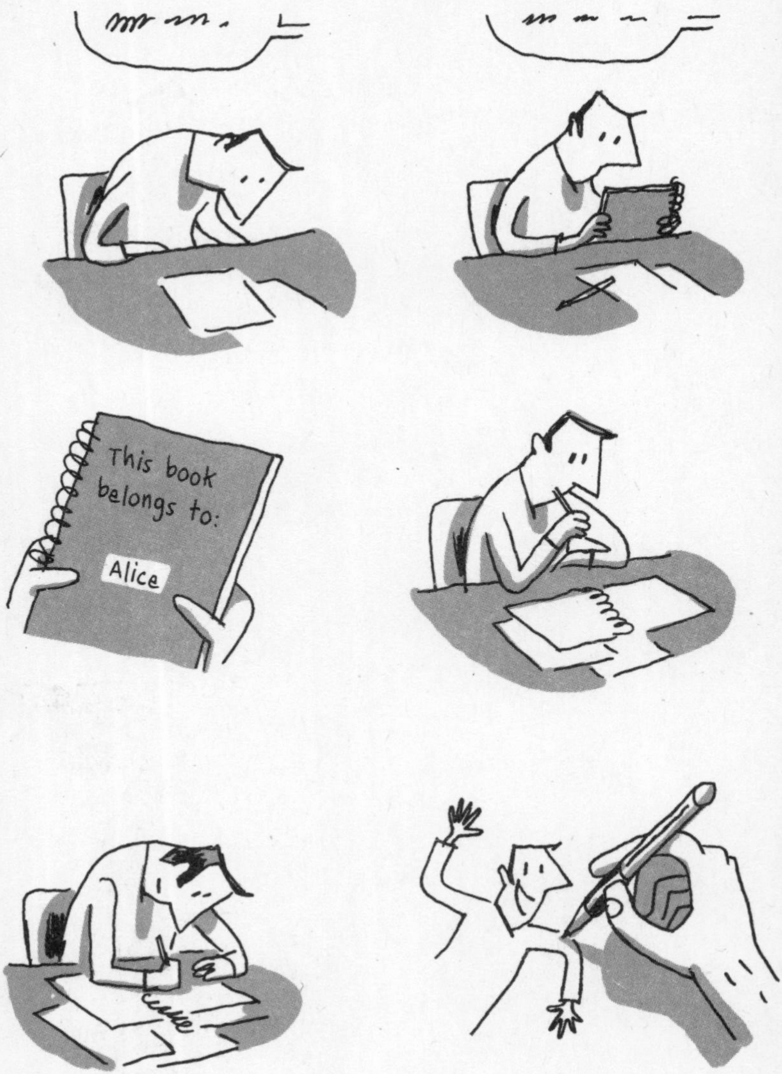
This book belongs to:
Alice

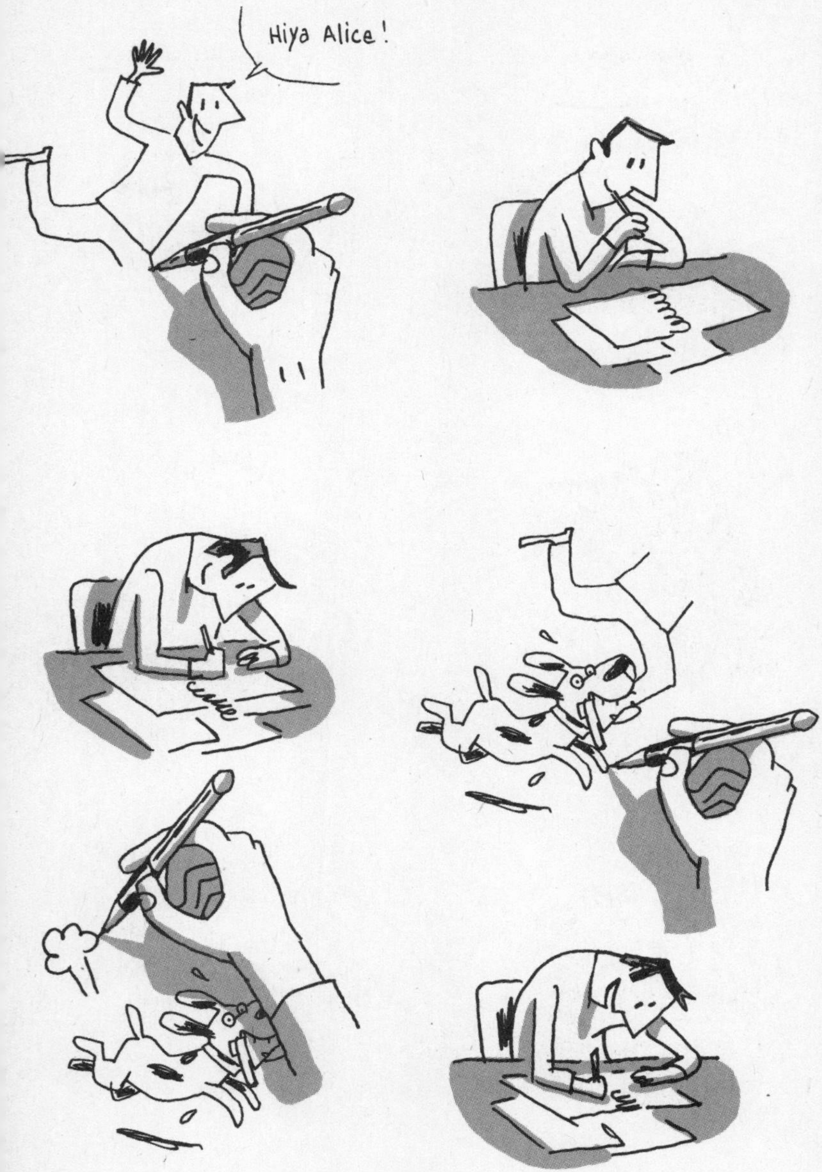
Hiya Alice!

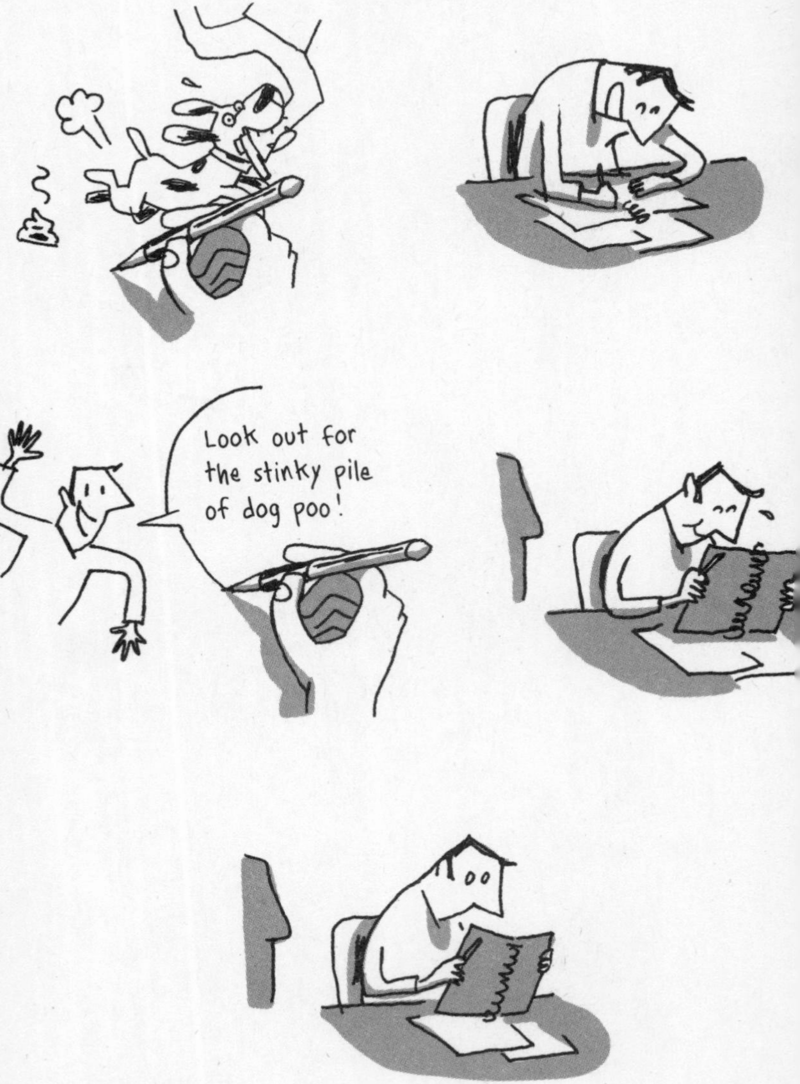
Look out for the stinky pile of dog poo!

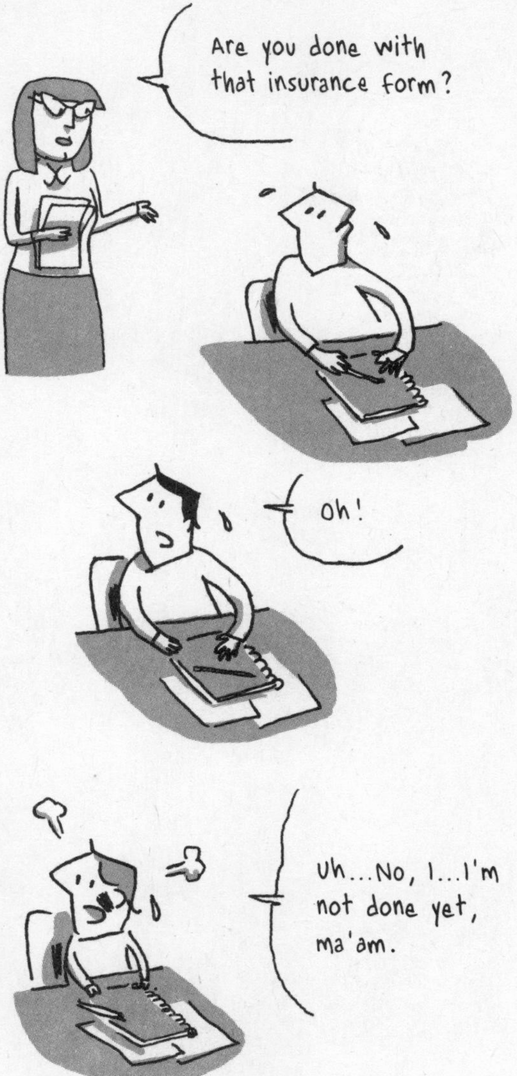
Are you done with that insurance form?
Oh!
Uh...No, I...I'm not done yet, ma'am.
DELISLE 2013

-Punctuality

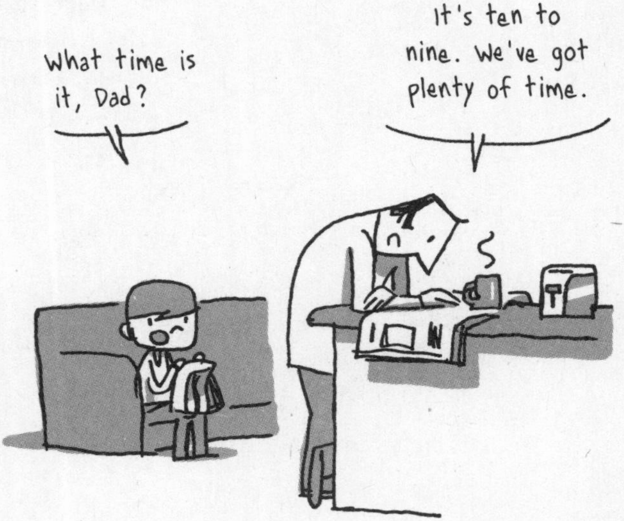
What time is it, Dad?
It's ten to nine. We've got plenty of time.

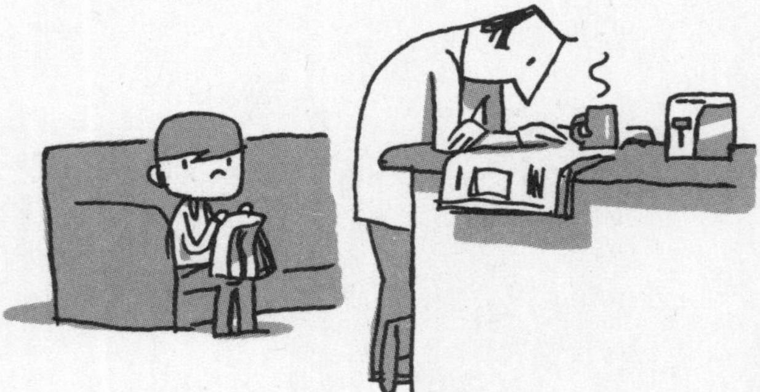

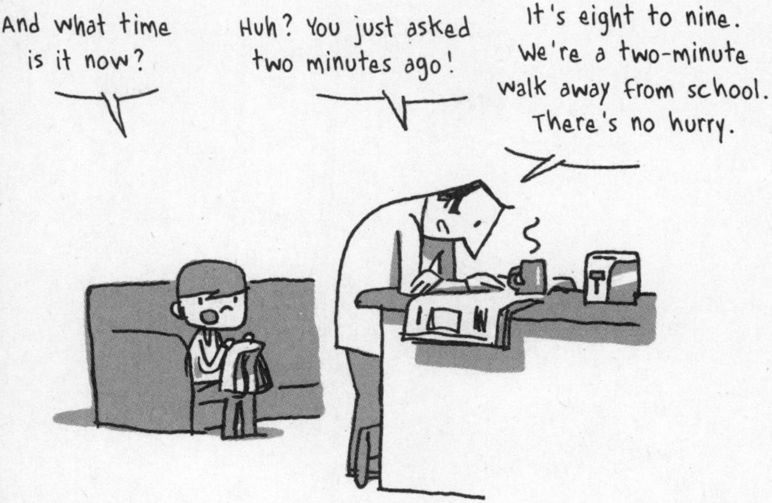
And what time is it now?
Huh? You just asked two minutes ago!
It's eight to nine. We're a two-minute walk away from school. There's no hurry.

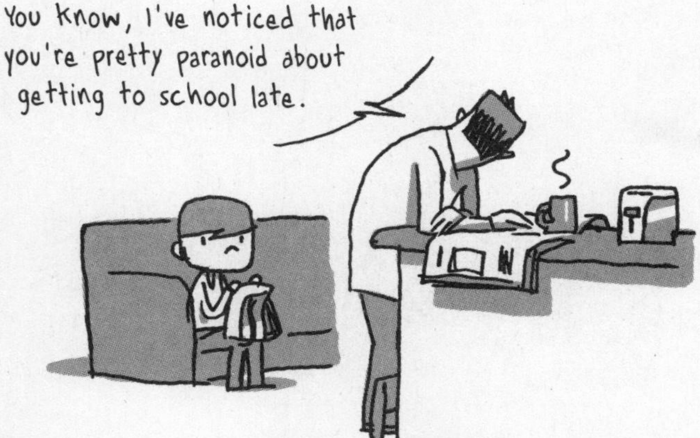
You know, I've noticed that you're pretty paranoid about getting to school late.

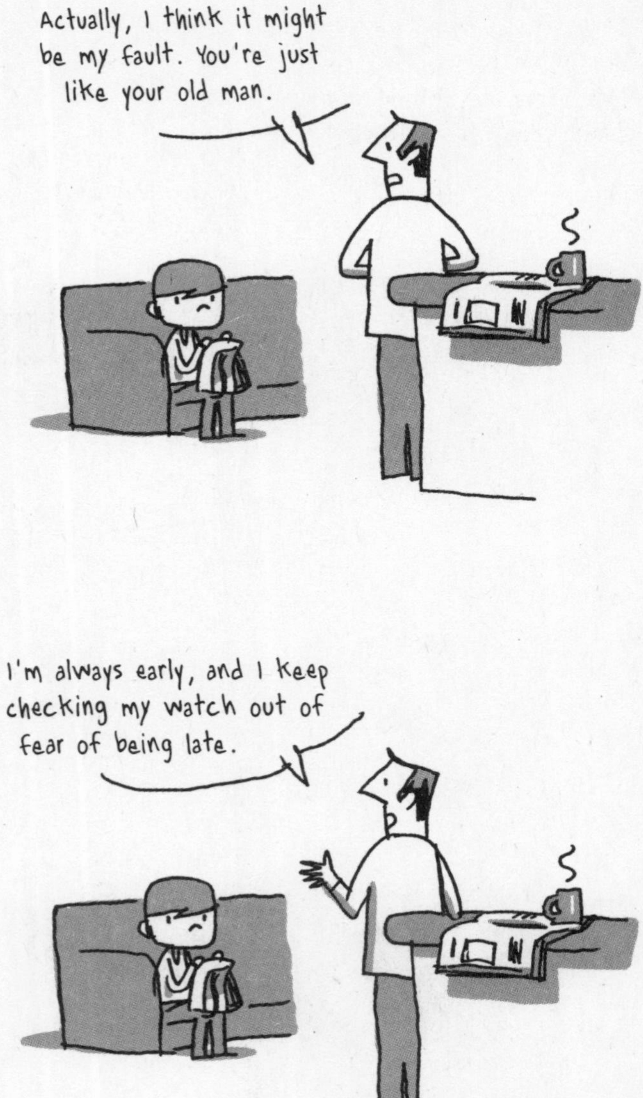
Actually, I think it might be my fault. You're just like your old man.
I'm always early, and I keep checking my watch out of fear of being late.

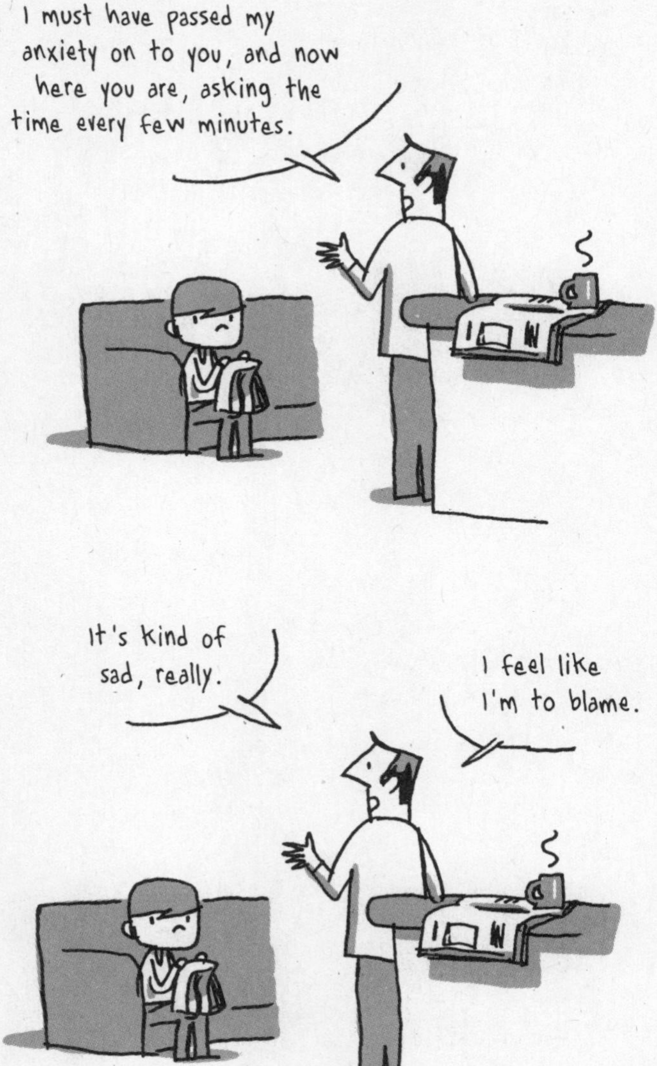
I must have passed my anxiety on to you, and now here you are, asking the time every few minutes.
It's kind of sad, really.
I feel like I'm to blame.

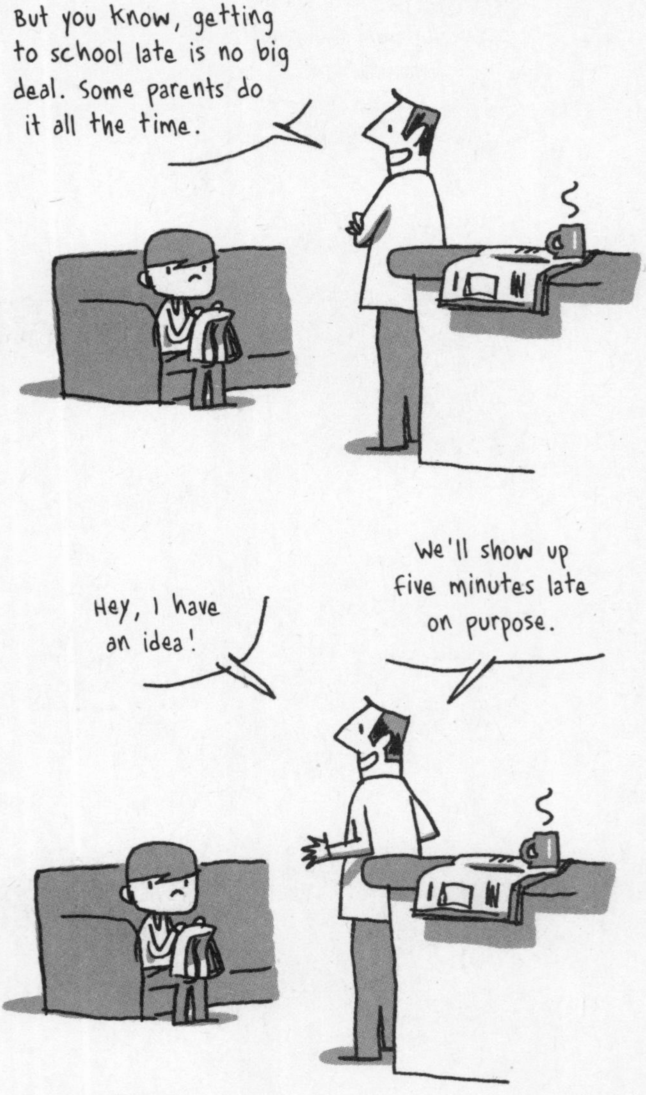
But you know, getting to school late is no big deal. Some parents do it all the time.
Hey, I have an idea!
We'll show up five minutes late on purpose.

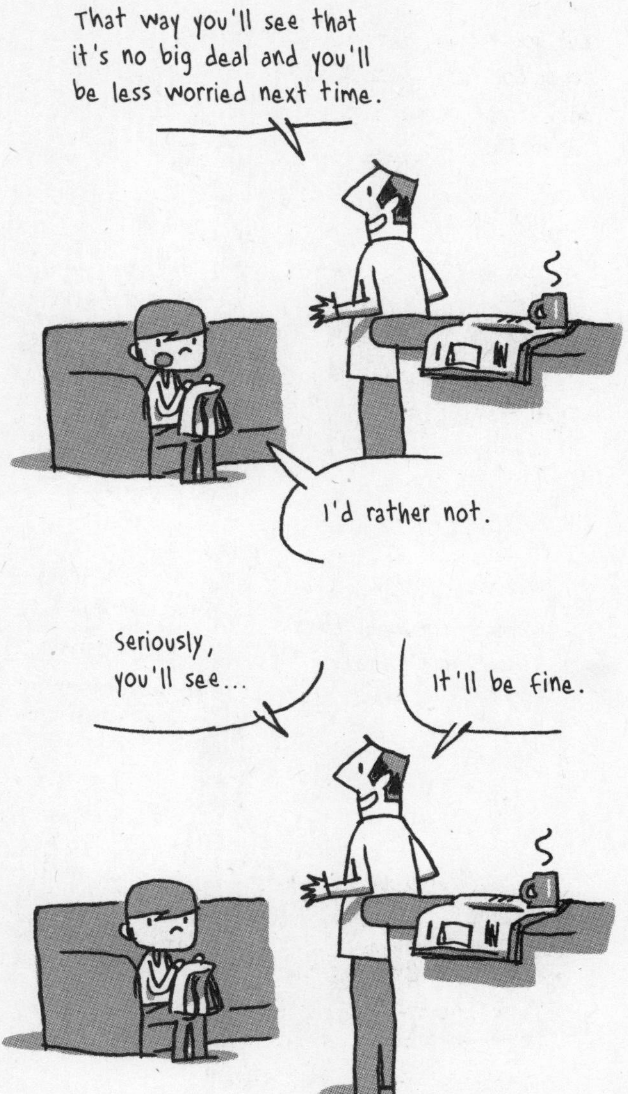
That way you'll see that it's no big deal and you'll be less worried next time.
I'd rather not.
Seriously, you'll see...
It'll be fine.

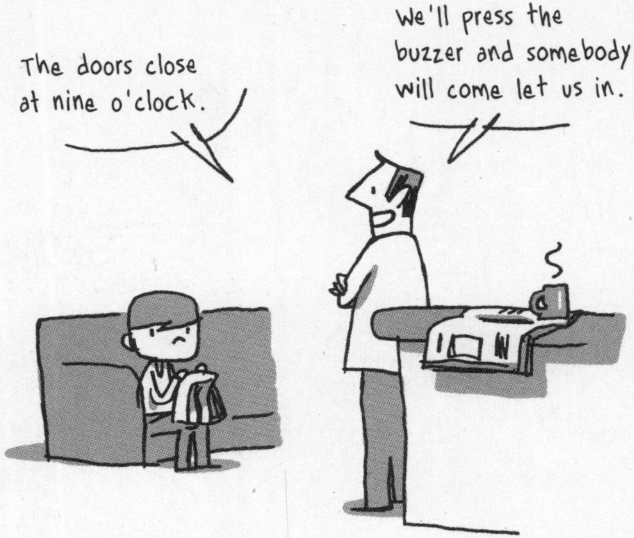
The doors close at nine o'clock.
We'll press the buzzer and somebody will come let us in.

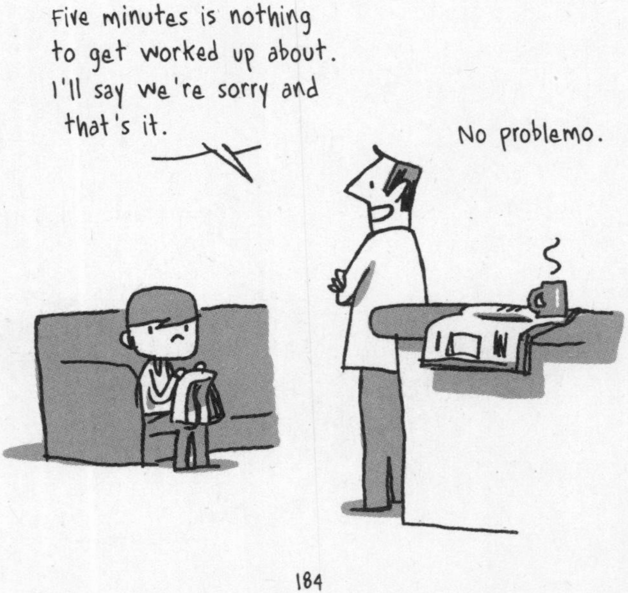
Five minutes is nothing to get worked up about. I'll say we're sorry and that's it.
No problemo.

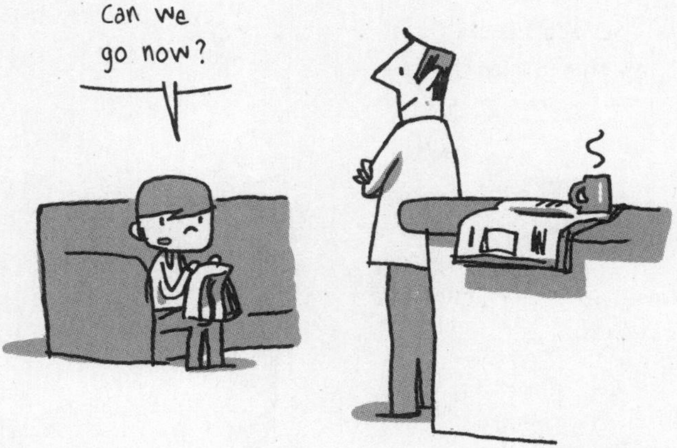
Can we go now?

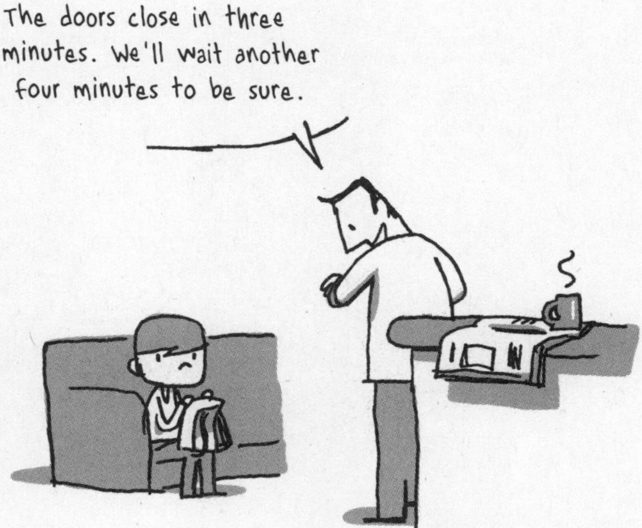
The doors close in three minutes. We'll wait another four minutes to be sure.

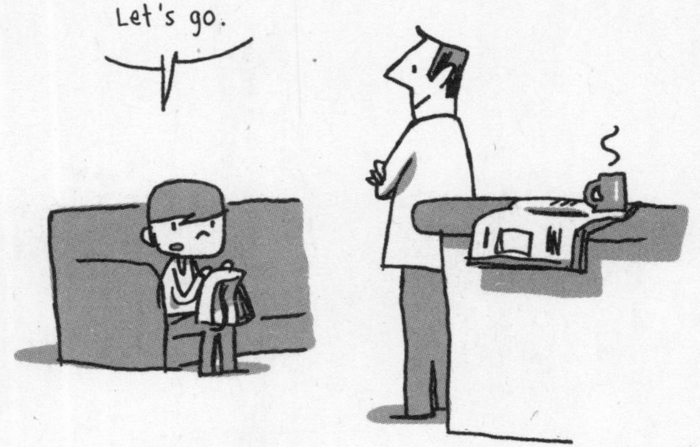
Let's go.

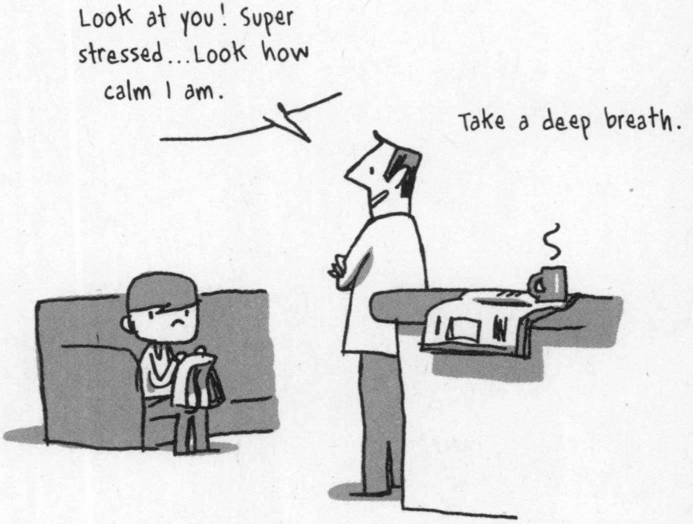
Look at you! Super stressed...Look how calm I am.
Take a deep breath.

I'm one hundred percent relaxed.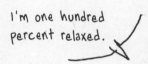

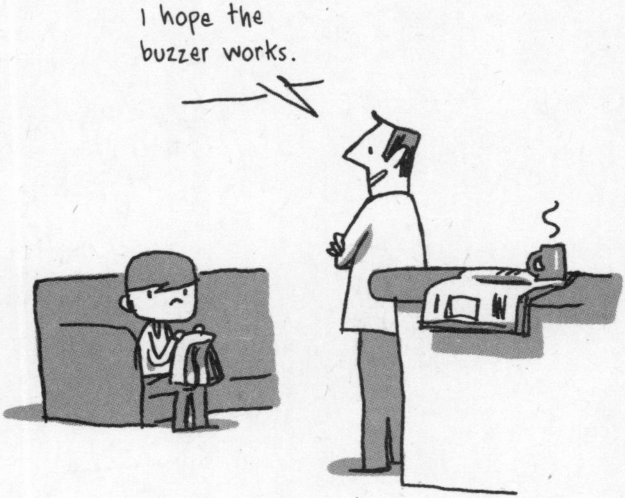
I hope the buzzer works.
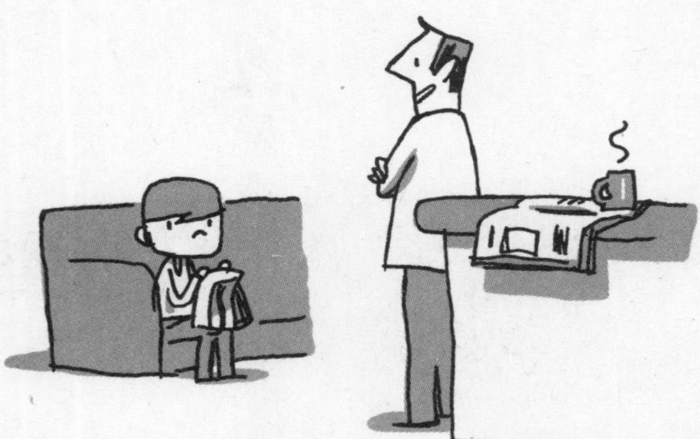

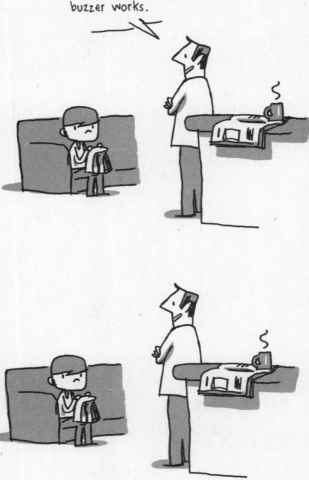

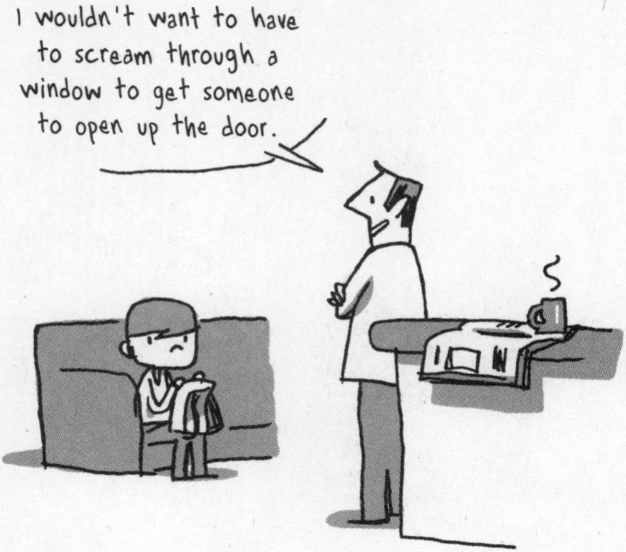
I wouldn't want to have to scream through a window to get someone to open up the door.

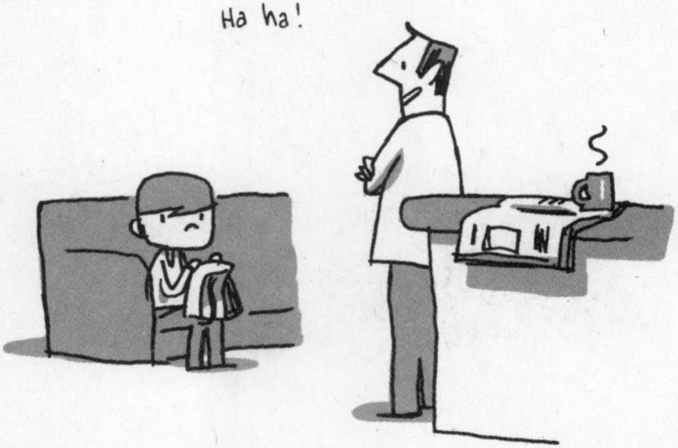
Ha ha!

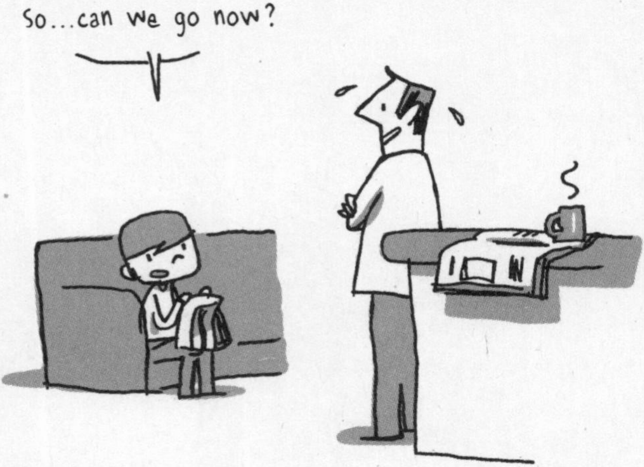
So...can we go now?

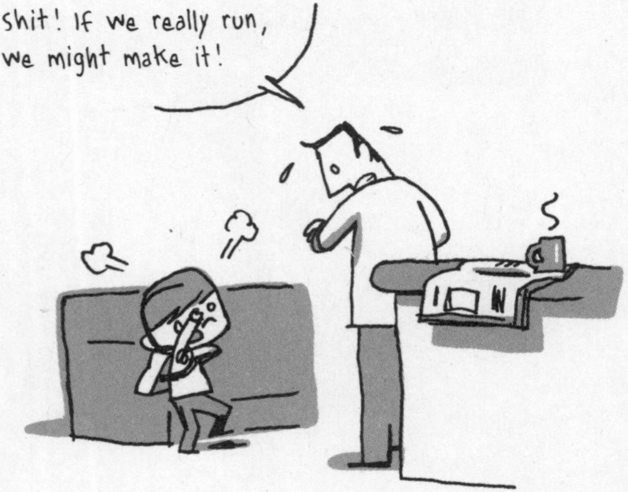
Shit! If we really run, we might make it!

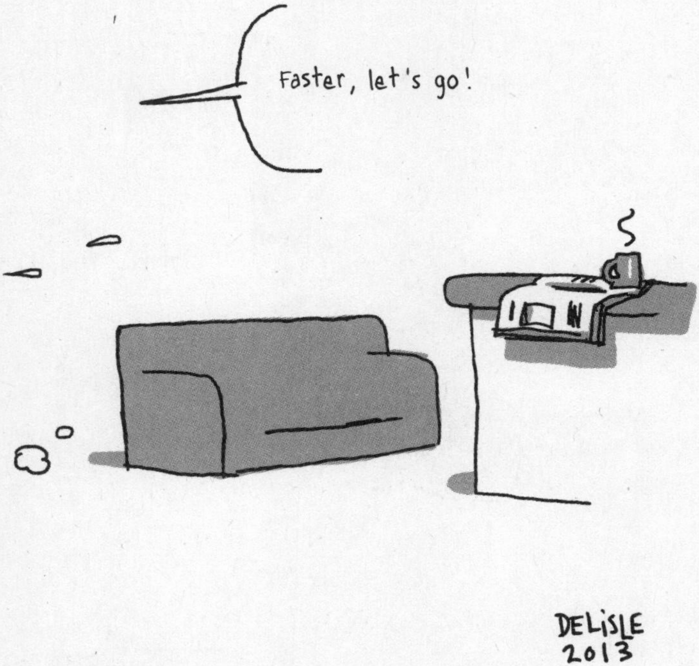
Faster, let's go!
DELISLE
2013